Rudy Bladel, Railway Killer

Ruth Kanton

Published by Trellis Publishing, 2021.

While every precaution has been taken in the preparation of this book, the publisher assumes no responsibility for errors or omissions, or for damages resulting from the use of the information contained herein.

RUDY BLADEL, RAILWAY KILLER

First edition. July 4, 2021.

ISBN: 979-8224135714

Written by Ruth Kanton.

RUDY BLADEL, RAILWAY KILLER

RUTH KANTON

Rudy Bladel

Rudy Bladel was born on December 8, 1932. His father, Holgar, was a railroad worker, employed by Chicago, Rock Island & Pacific Railroad Company. The family lived in the neighborhood around 67th Street and Ashland Avenue, and Bladel attended Chicago Vocational High School on the South Side. He took some automotive shop classes while in high school, and was planning on working for the railroad company like his father. After he graduated in June 1951, he found work with Rock Island, and was employed as a fireman. He joked about his job while talking to a Tribune journalist, stating, "That`s when you tossed coal in one end and you got smoke out the other."

Soon after, he enlisted in the army, and was assigned as a military engineer. He was deployed and served in the Korean War, where he was tasked with "hostling" locomotives in a South Korean roundhouse, sometimes even under enemy fire. After his service in Korea, Bladel made his way back home and was reemployed by Rock Island. He worked diligently, and made his way up the ranks as the years went by.

In 1959, a merger between two freight yards, one in Elkhart where Bladel worked, and another in Niles, Michigan, sparked major change. New York Central has decided to shift most of its operations from the Niles, Michigan, train yards, to the new rail yard in Elkhart. The decision resulted in more than 75 trainmen in Niles getting laid off, and train crews on the Niles seniority list were subsequently reduced from 22 to five. The changes sparked a number of issues, mainly how to redistribute the employees from the Elkhart and Niles yards. The railroad, as well as a court's decision, saw the unions scrambling to find a solution to this particular problem. Eventually, the unions came up with an agreement that the Elkhart yards staff would be composed of 52 percent of the Elkhart men, and the remaining 48 percent would be made up of the men from Niles. This split the groups into "Michigan boys" and "Elkhart men." A number of Elkhart men, including Bladel, were demoted, while others were fired.

To Bladel, this was unforgivable, and he was particularly angry at the "Michigan boys" who were "stealing their jobs." He constantly voiced his anger and dissent, and made frequent vows about making them pay for it. However, Rudy's colleagues didn't pay much attention to his words. No one really knew him well, since he spent most of his time alone. He was very quiet, and seemed to prefer keeping his own company even when others tried to befriend him. Whenever there were breaks as they worked, Bladel would disappear and turn up just before train time. If anyone asked where he had been, he would always mumble "I took a long walk," and carry on with his duties. A number of his colleagues stated that they had seen him talking to himself during his long walks.

Bladel was a bespectacled powerfully built man who was often described as moody and morose. He was fond of riding his motorcycle, and had been in an accident shortly after his army stint in Korea, which resulted in an unusual gait.

Unsolved Murders

Late in the night on Saturday, August 3, 1963, Virgil Terry, the 52 year old switchman for the Indiana Harbor Belt Railroad, punched in for work at the Hammond, Indiana, yard. The sprawling yards were where the crews assembled the massive freight trains for transport, usually heading east across Northern Indiana and Southern Michigan, or west towards Chicago, along the Belt, New York Central, and Conrail lines. Terry was on crew that night with 60-year-old Roy Bottorff as the engineer, and 45-year-old Paul Overstreet, the fireman. He knew that Overstreet and Borrtoff were waiting in the cab of the 55-car freight train that was awaiting clearance. Terry and some of his colleagues began working to coupling the engine to the train, and by the time they completed the job and pulled the train to the far end of the yard, it was 1:05 a.m. In his later statement to police, Terry said, "I got off the engine and walked to the west end switchman's shanty to call Hammond tower and get a clearance to get to the Calumet City yards. The tower man told me that we would have to wait for the Blue Island train to clear."

Terry waited for a few minutes, and watched as the Blue Island train cleared the Columbia Avenue crossing. He threw the switch to the main line, got his lantern and signaled for his engineer to come ahead. He recounted: "I did not get a return signal. As I walked toward my engine I gave the come ahead signal three or four times, and the engine did not move. I walked up to the side of the engine and I noticed Bottorff had his head laying part way out the side window. I climbed up on the engine and touched Roy on the arm, and then I noticed blood on his face and neck. I turned around and saw that Overstreet had blood on his face…"

Both men had died at the controls. They had each been shot twice in the back on the head, and three .22 caliber shell casing were recovered from the floor of the cab, and a fourth one on the ground next to the engine.

On August 6, 1968, at 4:38 a.m., shotgun blasts rung out in the rail yards at Elkhart, Indiana. 51-year-old John W. Marshall, an engineer, was found lying dead next to his diesel engine locomotive. He had been shot a total of four times – once in the side, once in the midsection, and twice in the head. The murder weapon was a 12-gauge weapon, and Marshall had been shot at close range.

Eight years later, on April 5, 1976, 51-year-old James "Tiny" McCrory, an engineer at the Elkhart yards, was found dead in the cab of his locomotive. McCrory, a resident of Niles, was in the locomotive, which was parked near the diesel house, when he was shot in the head with a deer slug, which was determined to have come from the barrel of a 20-gauge shotgun.

Sole Survivor

The McCrory murder had police wondering whether there was some truth to the stories about a phantom in the rail yards. Elkhart police sergeant David Keck, who was working on the Marshall and McCrory cases, took a closer look into the similarities surrounding both cases. Haunted by the possibility that they were looking for someone who had done this before, he sent out requests to other police departments along the railway line, looking for information on any other similar murders. It didn't take long for him to get the answers he was seeking. "When we checked with Hammond, they said, 'Yes, we had two killed in 1963,'" Keck recalled. The four murders were eerily similar – all four victims were trainmen who had been mysteriously gunned down in the pre-dawn hours while they were working in the switchyards. After pouring through the cases, Keck began searching for any other reports on any shootings that might have occurred in any of the train yards in the area, and he uncovered a report that no one had really paid much attention to since it was a simple open and shut case.

On March 30, 1971, Louis John Sayne was working in the Elkhart yards when he was shot twice in the back at around 3:55 a.m. Sayne, who had worked for New York Central as well as Contrail and Amtrak, recalled the attack: "I was in a happy mood because there were two train jobs that night and I got the good one, going to Chicago." He had just left an all-night restaurant after downing his cup of coffee, and was heading towards the roundhouse to climb into a freight engine when he heard two cracking sounds. Two bullets pierced his body, one slamming into his hip and the second one into his back. "I thought to run. But hell, I couldn't outrun bullets, so I turned around and faced him. We wrestled. He tripped on my overnight bag and fell down. I fell on top of him, grabbed the gun and shot him." The assailant was shot in the stomach.

The two men were rushed into the emergency room at Elkhart hospital, where surgeons promptly began working on them. As he lay on his hospital bed, Sayne looked over at the other man, and was surprised to see Bladel, who had crewed with him a couple of times in the past. Unable to contain his surprise, he asked Bladel: "Why did you shoot me, Rudy?" Bladel, who was 38 years old at the time, mumbled in response, "I did all I could to get the Niles men out of Elkhart."

Bladel was charged with attempted murder. However, he worked out a plea agreement with the prosecutors, and ended up pleading guilty to the lesser charge of aggravated battery. On December 31, 1971, he was sentenced to serve one to five years in the Indiana State Prison in Michigan. Bladel only served 18 months for his crime.

Sergeant Keck was convinced that Bladel may have had something to do with the other murders. The details of the Sayne shooting matched up with the other four scenes, and he reached out to the Hammond police to have their cases reopened. The detectives originally handling the Hammond cases had retired, so Keck elicited the help of Detectives Walter Murray and John Baron, and they reopened the cases. The three went through the case files again, and Keck recalled: "In Hammond there was a witness who had spotted this man (lurking in the switchyards) and said he walked 'like a gorilla' or had a 'farmer-type walk, like behind a plow, looking down at the ground.'" Thinking of Bladel's unusual gait, Keck stated, "That's Rudy. Then we went to the Marshall case, in which there were eyewitnesses. They couldn't put a face on the man but they put a walk on him and his build – Rudy Bladel. So we had our pattern. We made it a point to find out everything we could about Rudy Bladel."

Following his release from prison in 1973, Bladel, who had been fired after the Sayne shooting, appeared at a union hearing in a bid to get his fireman's job back. The appeal was unsuccessful. Speaking about the shooting, Bladel offered the explanation, "I only wanted to dust his pants off." Sayne attended the hearing, and was shocked when Bladel walked up to him afterwards, "He came up to me and shook my hand. He said his reason for shooting me had nothing to do with me personally, 'just the Michigan men.' Imagine that!"

Triple Homicide

After he was released from prison, Bladel was greatly feared by the railroad workers along the New York Central, Indiana Harbor Belt, and Conrail lines from northern Indiana to southern Michigan. They were well aware of their fallen colleagues, and kept a look out for Bladel whenever and wherever they worked. Richard Wheeler, a former Jackson police sergeant, stated: "Bladel knew the reputation he had among the railroad men, and he played on that. He would go up around the rail yards in Battle Creek, Kalamazoo and other towns just to stir them up. We know that for a fact." A number of trainmen complained: "He stalks the tracks. When you drive your train under a bridge, you look up and there's Rudy, staring down at you from the overpass."

Detectives followed up on Bladel's whereabouts during the Hammond shooting, and discovered that he had been living alone in a trailer in Blue Island at the time. One witness had told police that they heard a motorcycle leaving the scene following the shooting, and detectives were able to determine that Bladel owned a motorcycle. "We put a surveillance on him, a constant surveillance," Keck stated. The police surveillance caught Bladel buying a .357 magnum in South Bend, and they notified the Bureau of Alcohol, Tobacco, and Firearms (ATF). Bladel was arrested on January 6, 1978, and was sentenced to serve one to five years at the federal prison in Sandstone, Minnesota. On November 16, 1978, Bladel was released from prison. Sergeant Keck asked for the full-time surveillance on Bladel to be resumed, but this request was denied. Neither the department nor Conrail security had the necessary manpower to carry this out.

On December 31, 1978, at 6:44 p.m., six weeks after Bladel's release, three rail employees were found shot death at the Jackson, Michigan, depot. 50-year-old William Gulak, a conductor who lived in Lincoln Park, and 42-year-old Robert Lee Blake, a flagman from Southgate, were found in the trainmen's locker room at the depot. Both men were shot while they sat. The third victim, 32-year-old Charles Lee Burton, a fireman who lived in Jackson, was found on the loading platform outside the door. The men were killed by deer slugs from a 12-gauge shotgun. When Keck was informed of the murders, he told the officer on the other end of the line: "Find out where Rudy Bladel is!"

Investigation and Arrest

Jackson police began searching for Bladel, and they found him as he walked to a Greyhound bus station. He had spent the night in a hotel, and checked out early. He was taken into custody at 7 a.m. Police searched his suitcase, and inside they found newspaper clippings of the murders. He told police, "I figured I don't know what's going on here, but I figured I'd better get the heck out of here." He was questioned about the murders, and he told investigators that he had been at the depot earlier in the day, just to wash his hands. He maintained that he had been in Jackson looking for work, and he was released after 48 hours due to lack of evidence. By this time, police were focused on finding the murder weapon, and scuba divers were deployed to search the Grand River behind the train depot. Helicopters scoured the area looking for the weapon on rooftops, and police even consulted with psychics. The searches came up empty.

Three months later, the melting snow in the Cascade Falls Park revealed a shotgun hidden under one of the brushes. It had been broken down into two parts. Police were hoping that they had finally located the murder weapon. They compared the ejection marks on the test slugs fired from the recovered weapon to the slugs found at the scene of the murders. They matched. Investigators ran a search on the weapon's serial number, and it was traced back to Rudy Bladel. The gun had been bought from an Elkhart gun shop by Bladel, under his own name, on December 31, 1976, two years to the day of the Jackson murders.

On the afternoon of March 22, 1979, Jackson police made their way to Elkhart and arrested 45-year-old Rudy Bladel, who was living at a mission for homeless men. He was charged with three counts of murder and arraigned the next day, March 23. In court, the presiding judge told Bladel that he would appoint an attorney for him, and asked him not to speak to police without his legal representative present. When asked whether he understood the Miranda rights read to him, he replied in the affirmative. He pleaded not guilty to the charges, and he completed the forms requesting appointed counsel, at that time, or later in the day.

He told reporters at his arraignment, "I just don't know what to say," and then he smiled and posed for pictures.

Trial and Sentencing

According to Jackson police lieutenant Ronald Lowe, Bladel willingly confessed to the murders after he was confronted with the evidence police had – the recovered shotgun as well as the fiber particles found on the breech of the gun that matched fiber particles on his clothing and suitcase. Bladel supposedly stated, "You've got me. What do you want to know?"

Lieutenant Lowe recounted: "Bladel told me and Sgt. Gerald Rand that he left the hotel, went down to the depot carrying his suitcase with the shotgun in it, put the suitcase down on the platform, got his shotgun out, put it together, walked in the door (of the locker room), shot the man sitting beside the door (Blake), shot the man at the table (Gulak) and (then) put another slug into each of them. As he was going out, another man (Burton) started in the door and he shot that man and he fell on the platform."

While Bladel's letter of appointment was sent to a law firm on March 23, unbeknownst to him, it had not yet been received by Monday March 26, when he made his confession during an interrogation that took place while he was in the county jail. He had repeatedly asked for an attorney, but the officers who arrived to interrogate him that day had not been apprised of that fact. Bladel signed a waiver form after he granted the officers permission to proceed without his attorney present. He then went on to confess. His appointment letter was received by the law firm on March 27.

One of the officers testifying at trial told the court:

A: Mr. Bladel at that time stated that he had requested an attorney at his arraignment, but he hadn't seen him, seen the attorney yet, but he would talk to us, and he said he would talk to us, and he said he didn't need his attorney there while he was talking to us.

* * *

Q: Was there any mention of an attorney at that time?

A: I asked him if he desired his attorney present and he stated he did not need one.

Q: What, if anything, further took place then?

A: In addition to the last statement that Mr. Bladel said, when I asked him if he needed his attorney present he stated, 'I don't need him present. I am going to plead guilty anyway.'"

When his trial began in the summer, Bladel recanted his confession. In his testimony, he stated: "They (the police) were yelling at me, so I told them what they wanted to hear. They got me all confused and confumbled." He told the court that he had been in Jackson to retrieve his motorcycle, and that he had been in the area on the day of the murders "to use the trainmen's washroom." He admitted that he did own the shotgun used to commit the murders, but that he had sold it several weeks before the killings to a stranger in an Elkhart restaurant for $100. Part of the cross examination with Jackson County prosecutor Edward Grant went as follows:

Q: Did you have some grievance against the railroad company?

A: In the past, yes. They gave our jobs away. The Niles men took our jobs and laid us off.

Q: And it caused you to lose quite a bit of time?

A: Right, 524 days (between Oct. 16, 1959, and Nov. 14, 1964).

Q: Did you do different things to harass the railroad?

A: Like what, for instance?

Q: Would you go around and stare at railroad employees and just stand by the trains and stare at the trainmen and firemen, to make them feel uncomfortable?

A: I`ve stood at different places, just all kinds of places. I am sitting here and looking at you. Is this harassment?

The jury returned a guilty verdict, and on August 29, 1979, he was sentenced to serve three concurrent life terms.

Appeals and Retrial

Following his sentencing, Bladel filed motions appealing the verdict, and centered his appeals on the validity of his confession. The Court of Appeals affirmed Bladel's conviction, writing in part:

> The Court of Appeals rejected defendant's assertion that interrogation can never occur once a defendant requests counsel. The court acknowledged that the prosecutor bore a heavy burden in proving a knowledgeable and voluntary waiver and that the police may have acted unethically in obtaining the confession. Nevertheless, the waiver was valid because defendant had been warned by the Indiana magistrate not to talk to police until he met with counsel, he had prior contact with the criminal justice system and understood his rights, he had signed a waiver form, and had not reasserted his right to counsel during the interrogation. Finally, the four-day delay between arraignment and the first meeting with counsel was not unreasonable. There was no evidence that defendant was kept from his attorney in order to obtain a confession.

Following this rejection, Bladel filed an application for leave to appeal with the Michigan Supreme Court. The matter was remanded back to the Michigan Court of Appeals for reconsideration. The Michigan Court of Appeals concluded that it was compelled to reverse Bladel's conviction, citing "the issue of violation of right to counsel in the context of an interrogation occurring after a defendant has requested the appointment of counsel." The Michigan Supreme Court upheld the decision, concluding that Bladel's "right to counsel had been infringed."

Bladel was retried for the murders, and this time the confession was not presented in court. On June 19, 1987, he was once again convicted on three counts of first degree pre-meditated murder and sentenced to life in prison.

Civil Lawsuit

On January 19, 1979, following the murders of Robert Lee Blake, Richard Lee Burton, and William Gulak, the families of Blake and Burton filed a lawsuit against Consolidated Rail Corporation, Conrail, and the National Railroad Passenger Corporation, Amtrak, in the Jackson Circuit Court. The plaintiffs asserted that "Conrail's legal duty was to provide Blake and Burton with a safe workplace, and that Conrail also had a duty to protect Blake and Burton from Bladel's criminal assault against them during the course of their employment." They presented Bladel's past vendetta against railroad workers, including the open murder cases that Bladel was suspected of committing. They also presented evidence that sergeant Keck had been in the Elkhart yards a number of times, and that he had warned Conrail employees that Bladel was out of prison and that he would kill again.

The plaintiffs maintained that Conrail knew about Bladel's vendetta, and that they still failed to implement security measures to protect its employees. No warnings were given by the company, even though Conrail officer Long had written in his November 18, 1978, report that "Rudy Bladel is back in town," after he was released from prison, and that he still held a grudge against anyone connected with the railroad.

Conrail and Amtrak fought against the lawsuit, claiming that they were not liable for the deaths of Blake and Burton. They filed motions to suppress Bladel's past from being introduced as evidence, which was upheld by the Michigan Court of Appeals. However, the summary judgment was later reversed, and the plaintiffs filed for a transfer of venue to the Wayne Circuit Court.

This motion was granted, and the matter moved to trial, which lasted six weeks.

The plaintiffs were finally granted $4,500,000 by the circuit court in the motion against Conrail, and $4,400,000 against Amtrak. The defendants appealed, but the Michigan Court of Appeal did not find any merit in their claims of error.

Death

While Bladel maintained that his was innocent even following his second conviction, the railroad murders ceased after his arrest in 1979. Investigators tried getting him to confess to the four unsolved murders – Roy Borttof, Paul Overstreet, John Marshall, and James McCrory – hoping that his life sentence had made him a little bit more forthcoming. Former Hammond detective John Baron asked Bladel to help him solve the Hammond murders, stating, "Look, Rudy, you are doing life. What have you got to lose?" Bladel's reply was "You're a cop. Prove I did it."

Rudy Bladel died on November 15, 2006, from thyroid cancer while hospitalized in the Henry Ford Allegiance Health Hospital in Jackson.

Murder at the Charisma Ranch

Robert Dorotik was born in 1945, two years before his future wife Jane Marguerite Colvey. It would be 23 years before they would meet and fall in love. They married on April 4, 1970 in Los Angeles California.

Two years later Nicholas was born, another son Alexander would follow shortly after that and by January 16, 1976 their family would be complete with the birth of their daughter Claire Elizabeth.

Robert was an Engineer and Jane was a Health care professional as well as a successful business woman. She made a six figure salary from her 9-5 job alone, and the horse ranch she ran with her daughter was starting to bring in money too.

Robert and Jane would have more than one argument over the money Jane and their daughter Claire spent on Charisma Ranch. He quit his job as an engineer to support Jane's endeavor of raising and training horses. Bob started a business making horse jumps, but by 2000 his business was in trouble. One of the last arguments Jane and Bob had was when Jane and Claire told him they found another horse that would be perfect for the ranch. Robert complained they didn't need any more horses. This infuriated Jane and she told him in no uncertain terms that it was her money and she would spend it how she wanted, she didn't need his permission.

On the afternoon of February 13, 2000 Jane got ready to go down to tend to the horses. Bob was dressing in his jogging clothes and told Jane he was going to go for a run. Bob had been a long distance runner for years. Jane had an injury that prevented her from participating. Jane asked her husband to stoke the fire before he left and she went to the barn.

Mrs. Dorotik returned to the house a couple hours later and Bob was nowhere to be found. She waited a while longer and began looking for him. There were others including neighbors and sons Nick and Alex. Becoming increasingly worried about her husband Jane called the police and told them that he had not come home after his run. A search was organized by the police and in the early morning hours of February 14, 2000 Police found Robert's battered, bloodied body by the side of the road about three miles from home. Police immediately suspected Jane.

Robert Dorotik had died from blunt force trauma and strangulation. He had several injuries to the face and the back of the head (an expert testified the wounds were consistent with a hammer). There were defensive wounds on his hands. He was still wearing his jogging clothes although according to the detectives his shoes were tied in an odd manner. The rope used to strangle him was still around his neck and had made a laceration on his throat.

They did not find blood at the scene that would have been consistent with it being the murder site. Robert had been killed somewhere else and moved here. They found the tire tracks and shoe prints. Jane could not be linked to any of the shoe prints, only the tire tracks. However, hers were not the only tire tracks there, the others were not linked to anyone.

The evidence from the beginning seemed to point at Jane Dorotik as the killer. At the scene where they found the body there were tire tracks that matched the three different treads on her truck. At the residence there was a massive amount of blood that had been cleaned at. Jane claims that the blood was from a nosebleed Robert had and cleaned up. Between the box springs and mattress there was a towel soaked with blood. In a bag in the master bedroom they found a syringe with a horse tranquilizer in it and Jane's fingerprint in Bob's blood was found on it. She was arrested before the blood analysis could even be returned.

Around the room investigators found impact blood spatter patterns as well as drip, transfer and cast off. In one of the closets in the house they found a steam carpet shampooer and a significant amount of cleaning supplies. Bob's blood was found on the cap, handle and nozzle of one of the bottles.

Blood stains consistent with Robert's were found in the bed of the truck Jane, Claire and the ranch hands used around the ranch. They found no blood spatter on his shoes or shirt, but did find some blood on his boxers. One of the two hands never showed up for work the day after Bob's death.

Jane was booked into San Diego County Jail and with the help of family made bail.

Jane's daughter Claire was incriminated in the murder, that she was actually the one that killed Robert, her own father. It was well known that father and daughter had a stormy relationship, and at times became volatile. It was never revealed why the two seemed to hate each other, but Claire even wrote a scathing letter to her father about a "betrayal of trust."

Jane's defense team Kerry Steigerwalt and Cole Casey now had to figure out how to defend their 55 year old client. What they decided on wasn't the most unusual way to do it and it and many other attorneys had done in numerous courtrooms around the country. They deliberately brought Claire up as a suspect. By showing that another person 'could' have committed the murder there is a chance that it will raise enough of a doubt in a jury's mind for them to bring back an acquittal instead of a guilty verdict. This is what the attorney's for Jane were doing, trying to raise a reasonable doubt. This strategy would ultimately tear the family apart. In a letter written three years after her conviction Jane would call her attorney 'ego driven' and the implicating of her daughter a 'seriously flawed defense strategy.'

Prosecutor Bonnie Howard-Regan was convinced that Jane killed her husband to keep from having to pay him spousal support. It seemed there was an impending divorce on the horizon for Bob and Jane. They had separated in 1997 but talked it out and decided to keep their money separate and got back together.

Their own sons commented that their parents' marriage wasn't the most loving and at times their fights became very heated. But is this a motive for murder? Perhaps not just the fights, maybe it was the fact that if the two divorced Jane would have to pay Robert up to 40% of her annual income. This would be upwards of 50,000 dollars a year. Jane was incensed when a divorce attorney had told her that. That is a huge motive for murder in the eyes of the law. There was also a $250,000 life insurance policy on both Bob and Jane. She was forthcoming with the detectives about this during the investigation. If she had to pay that much out in spousal support she wouldn't be able to keep the horse ranch, and it seemed that was all she cared about.

Jane's trial would begin in May of 2001 a little over a year after her husband was murdered. Jane had pled not guilty and was making passionate pleas to the public declaring her innocence. Though her daughter and sister also claimed that Jane was innocent of this heinous crime, Claire, Bonnie Long and a ranch hand all invoked their Fifth Amendment right against self-incrimination. Steigerwalt brought up the fact that Claire's alibi was never confirmed. Had the Sheriff's Department zeroed in on Jane in a hasty attempt to close the case?

On June 9, 2001 the case of Jane Dorotik v The State of California went to the jury for deliberation. After the third day both the defense and the prosecution were starting to worry. Maybe they hadn't presented their case as well as they'd thought. Maybe they didn't explain things in an easy to understand way. In the end however, it wasn't that the jury had a problem understanding what they saw and heard during the trial. They were just being diligent, making sure every juror understood what the evidence was and how it fit in the scheme of things. In fact, they had a unanimous decision on the first vote...guilty on the charge of first degree murder.

Judge Joan Weber said that there was "an overwhelming amount of circumstantial evidence" and when Jane's attorney filed for a new trial it was denied. New witnesses had come forward and Steigerwalt asked that the case be reopened to the jury could hear what they had to say. She denied his request. Weber also asked, "How could you have your husband's blood on your hands if you had nothing to do with his death?" The Judge Weber was referring to the syringe with Janes fingerprint on it. It was an integral piece of evidence in the case.

Without a new trial in San Diego County, the next step is Court Of Appeal Of California, Fourth Appellate District, Division One.

The Court of Appeals works differently than the Trial Court. It is not a place for a new trial or a retrial. They won't look at new evidence or hear from new witnesses. It is strictly for trying to overturn the lower court's decision. If this happens then the Trial Court would be made to do one of several different actions in the case. One would be a whole new trial, which in Jane's case is what her attorney would want to happen. Or perhaps the Appellate Court would order Trial Court to look at additional evidence and/or revisit the facts in the case.

Either of these would be a win for Jane and her defense team. However, before these could happen her attorney would have to show that there was an error in the trial procedure or in how Weber interpreted the law.

This all starts with a Notice to Appeal, and then a brief has to be filed. In many cases appeals are decided based solely on this brief. Other times there will oral arguments before anything is decided.

Janes appeal was filed on November 18, 2003. She is asserting that Judge Weber should have included in the instructions to the jury the lessor charge of voluntary manslaughter because the state didn't present evidence that there was premeditation and aforethought to constitute first degree murder. She was denied.

On June 12, 2009 Jane filed another appeal. There were three key facts in this appeal. In the first one she claims 'ineffective assistance of counsel'. Jane claimed that her defense team didn't represent her properly. They didn't do any investigation of their own.

Second, she believed that not letting the jury hear from the new witnesses and not doing DNA testing jeopardized her case. The rope used to strangle Robert was never test for DNA, claiming that epithelia's of the real killer would have been found.

Third, there were procedural mistakes because of the delayed discovery and her actual innocence.

The defense was not allowed to present evidence that the State's expert witness had many mistakes in other cases by using 'faulty methodology'. The jury was not allowed to hear from an eyewitness.

The Appellate Court denied her, again.

The San Diego Union-Tribune reported on November 22, 2015 that a Judge has determined Jane be allowed to have the DNA in her case tested. The rope used to strangle Bob, the fingernail scrapings, and a piece of hair found around the victim's finger all be tested.

Jane still proclaims her innocence and said the ranch hand that didn't show up for work the day after the murder should be considered. He drives a black pick-up, and his tire tracks were also found at the scene. She also reiterated that the man owed the Dorotik's money.

Jane filed her first appeal on November 18, 2003. The Appellate court upheld the lower court's decision. Then Jane, known also as the petitioner filed Habeas petition on April 4, 2006 in the State Superior Court. Next was a Habeas Petition in the Appellate Court on January 3, 2006. And again Jane filed with the State Supreme Court on November 20, 2006. All appeals and motions to this point had been denied or affirmed the lower court's decision.

On June 1, 2007 Jane would file a Petition for Writ of Habeas Corpus, a Motion to appoint counsel, a Motion for Leave to Proceed in Forma Pauperis and a request for DNA testing. This too was denied or dismissed.

In July of 2007 Jane managed to get the money for filing fees and Magistrate Judge Porter ordered the case be reopened on July 9, 2007.

In the appeal for ineffectual assistance of counsel the superior court "denied the claims on the merits in a written order but only addressed the first two claims. On appeal the Appellate Court did the same thing.

Jane contends that council should have done independent testing of the forensic evidence that the prosecution would be presenting at trial and that there was other available evidence that he could have taken advantage of but didn't. Jane contends that had he done so the findings would have weakened the prosecution's case.

Another point the petitioner brought up is that her counsel didn't call her as a witness in her own defense.

Petitioner wanted a medical professional called as an expert witness to testify as to the medical impossibility that she could have perpetrated the murder due to an injury from an accident years earlier. That she would not have had the strength to do what the prosecution says she did.

Counsel for the defense did not object when a detective testified that he thought she was the killer. He could have also asked for a mistrial also.

He didn't insist on DNA testing prior to the start of the trial, armed with the results of the tests, petitioner is sure that it would have pointed to the real killer or killers.

Petitioner believes that her counsel should have brought up different scenarios that could have explained away the circumstantial evidence brought up at trial.

That he could have provided innocent theories for the incriminating evidence.

He didn't show that police didn't follow any leads, including eyewitnesses that came forward in the early stages of the investigation; they made up their mind that she was guilty. Therefore they didn't look for the real killer/killers.

Jane contends that her counsel could have done their own investigation and found the witnesses that were not heard at trial. Instead he made the leap to blaming Claire Dorotik as a defense.

And finally, follow through on the promises counsel made to the jury about what the evidence would show, and not make a comment to the affect that Jane was guilty.

If none of these ten points were true but the last one, would that fact that her own defense counsel made a comment that directly or indirectly told the jury he thought she was guilty should have been grounds for a mistrial and perhaps proceedings started to disbar her attorney.

The points brought up in Jane's eyes caused her to be wrongly convicted for the murder of her husband.

The forensic evidence in many parts does not support the prosecution's theory. Think about the "blood" found on the wall that supposedly dripped down from the master bedroom upstairs. The man who sold /rented the property to the Dorotik's knew of a water leak. Rain water would get in the track of the sliding door and seep down the wall of the stairs leading to the bedroom. There was Bob's DNA there, but was it from blood? Walking shirtless up the stairs and rubbing his sweaty arm on the wall could leave his DNA, it was not said that it was blood.

Post-conviction reports showed that there was way less blood present than would have been if the State's expert witness, Merrit, were correct. McDonell who did the post-conviction report says the fatal blow probably occurred outside the bedroom. But at the same time doesn't accept the idea that Bob was killed where he was found or that he was killed somewhere else, body dumped where it was found and the blood evidence planted.

McDonell also said that the blood on the mattress could have easily been caused by a bloody nose. That being said it still doesn't explain the different blood stain patterns found throughout the room.

Those where found on the pillow, nightstand, walls, bedspread and the window. Those he said cannot be explained away by a nosebleed.

The post-conviction report says that Merrit's testimony was wrong inasmuch as there was not enough blood soaked in to support his idea that Bob remained on the mattress for a long time after the attack.

McDonell concurs with petitioner that the blood around the pot-belly stove could very well have been from the nosebleed. Petitioner wants further testing to find out if it even had anything to do with the murder at all.

The bloody thumb print on the syringe was due to Bob helping Jane with a vet procedure. There was a horse tranquilizer inside the syringe and Jane's thumbprint in Bob's blood on it. This was admitted into evidence? Why, it's said to be a 'key piece' of evidence in the prosecution's case. Petitioner's counsel didn't object? Per Bob's toxicology report there was no drugs in his system. How did they tie it into the murder?

The truck, tire tracks and shoe prints. There was much to do about the tire tracks at the scene where Bob's body was found. There were actually two sets, one belonging to the family truck, the one that everyone including the farm hands had access to. But there was another set, never identified. The shoe prints found also at the scene couldn't be attributed to Jane either. Both sets were too big. The tracks that showed Jane's truck had backed up at the spot where the body was found can easily be explained as well. Bob used the truck to measure jogging routes. If he were to come to the exact length he wanted, he would have just turned around at that spot, hence the backup tracks.

A cursory search of the house was done the evening that Jane reported Bob missing. Police and Police dogs were all in the house including the master bedroom. They didn't find any blood.

Jane was in an accident in 1983 and had a severe injury to a hip which had to be put back together with metal and screws. The prosecution says that Jane would have bludgeoned her husband, then carried him down the stairs from the bedroom, through the house, across a 60' porch and lifted him into the back of a full sized Ford F250. Defense counsel should have brought up the fact that his client couldn't have done any of that. The Appellate court says that her sons saw her pulling irrigation pipes around the ranch that weighed about 75 lbs. pulling on 75lbs of something is different than lifting 147 lbs of dead weight.

Detective Richard Empson when questioned about the rope used to strangle Robert Dorotik and why it wasn't tested for DNA said the "criminologists in his office discouraged testing it because too many people had handled it." When pressed about the possibility of DNA on it that could have belonged to Claire or the ranch hand Leonel Morales or someone else and lead to the real killer, what then? Empson continued, "I believe I know who killed Bob Dorotik, that's why I arrested Jane Dorotik." Personal opinions are not supposed to be brought in to testimony, especially from an officer of the court. Did Jane's counsel object to this? Did it prejudice the jury against the petitioner? It could be said that it inflamed the jury. Most jurors will believe a law enforcement officer over anyone else. Even if the comment was objected to and stricken from the record the juror's still heard it and no matter if they are told to disregard it, it will still be in their mind.

There are so many points that Jane brought up on each one of her appeals. And each and every one of them were dismissed by the Courts. Many of Jane's friends and family still believe that Jane is innocent and should at least get a new trial so all of the evidence can be heard and that maybe she can even testify in her own defense. Although her trial court attorney believed that doing so was not a good idea. Clearly he didn't believe his client was innocent of the crime.

In the findings of the Appellate Court they say that the petitioner didn't show how not having the jury hear that Merrit's methodology was flawed and that he had been wrong on other cases would not have changed the jury's verdict.

They stated that even though the petitioner believes that the prosecution purposefully did not test for DNA she cannot prove how it would have changed anything. Also added the testing would not have brought forth any exculpatory or impeaching evidence. Knowing that DNA has set wrongfully convicted people free by proving their innocence this statement seems wrong in its entirety. Jane would be in a Catch 22 scenario, she can't prove that by not testing there was an error in law and without being able to prove it would help her case they wouldn't allow the testing.

Jane says she's been through a living hell since being sent to Chowchilla's prison facility in central California. But she hasn't been wasting her time. Along with filing the above mentioned appeals she is fighting for her fellow prisoners who are over the age of 55.

Jane is appalled at how many women are incarcerated and how the number keeps growing every year. She was once a mental health professional and says that a large number of women in prison should be in a Mental Health facility.

According to Jane "Medical care is liken to a third world country." And "there are women dying in prison alone and unnoticed by prison staff.

What she is trying to get done is this, have more compassionate releases, the parole board has the authority to do this but won't. So a program is working its way through legislation in the state of California. "If The Risk Is Low, Let Them Go".

Jane isn't advocating opening the flood gates and letting these women head off to parts unknown. There are a certain set of criteria in place to make sure the risk is actually low.

First of all, they have to have served at least 50% of their sentence or seven years.

They can't have had any disciplinary actions in the past five years. In other words they have to be a model prisoner.

They cannot have any other felony convictions of their record and they must have a concrete, safe place to stay in the community

These are safeguards to keep reoffenders inside the prison walls. Jane is very passionate about this program. She has watched many of what she calls "Golden Girls" languishing with terminal illnesses for years, alone, not able to be with family because Chowchilla houses inmates from all over the state.

Many of the families just don't have the money or time to be able to travel to see their loved ones. And even the children have to be patted down before they can go in to see a relative, to possibly say a last goodbye.

Jane's alternative custody program has to clear through law makers and with the help of different advocates it's headed in the right direction thanks to Carol Lui a senator from California.

This is being heralded as a great program to help with overcrowding of the prisons in California, and if this comes about in a timely manner it could help Jane as well. She is now 68 years old.

THE HILLSIDE STRANGLERS

NAOMI ROBERTS

Cousins Kenneth Bianchi and Angelo Buono, Jr. are collectively known by their media epithet "The Hillside Strangler". These two men were responsible for the murders of at least nine females, ages 12 to 28, during the late 1970s in Los Angeles, California, and Bianchi killed two more in Washington. After their first three victims did not gain much attention because they were prostitutes, Bianchi and Buono decided to abduct and murder middle-class "nice" girls. Five victims were found on hillsides in the Glendale-Highland Park area during Thanksgiving weekend in 1977 and the resulting panic led to the coining of the moniker "Hillside Strangler".

Lead Los Angeles Police Department homicide investigator Detective Sergeant Bob Grogan, along with his partner Dudley Varney as well as Los Angeles Sheriff's Department's Detective Frank Salerno, believed that the murders were the work of more than one killer but figured the less the murderers knew about what police knew the better.

Bianchi later moved to Washington where he murdered two more women before being caught.

Both Bianchi and Buono were convicted of multiple counts of first-degree murder and sentenced to life. Buono dies of a heart attack on 21 September 2002 while serving his time in Calipatria State Prison in Calipatria, California. Bianchi continues to serve his sentence at Washington State Penitentiary in Walla Walla.

Early Lives

Kenneth Bianchi

Kenneth Alessio Bianchi was born on 22 May 1951 in Rochester, New York, to a 17-year-old alcoholic prostitute who gave him up for adoption two weeks after he was born. He was adopted by Nicholas Bianchi and Frances Sciolono and despite a stable upbringing, Bianchi became a pathological liar at a very early age. Further, as a result of petit mal seizures he suffered at the age of five, Bianchi often daydreamt as if he were in a trance.

Bianchi suffered from insomnia and frequently wet the bed as a child (one of the triad symptoms of serial killers). Frances took him to the doctor on multiple occasions for his urination problem and being examined by the doctor caused Bianchi much embarrassment and humiliation. He also had a bad temper and was diagnosed with passive-aggressive personality disorder which is characterized by an individual who may appear to be enthusiastic about and actively comply with others' desires and needs while simultaneously resisting them, thus resulting in increased anger and hostility. At the core of this disorder is that the sufferer resents responsibility and instead of openly expressing his or her feelings, demonstrates said resentment through actions such as procrastination, forgetfulness, and inefficiency. Despite having a rather high IQ of 116, Bianchi was a chronic underachiever in school. When Frances took him to a psychologist, it was determined that Bianchi was overly dependent upon his mother.

On 2 January 1957, Bianchi fell off of a jungle gym and landed on his face. His mother then sent him to a private Catholic elementary school where he excelled in creative writing. In July 1963, Bianchi pulled down a six-year-old girl's pants after "spontaneously decid[ing] that he liked doing so".

His adoptive father died in 1964, thus leaving an unemotional Bianchi having to attend public high school where he joined a motorcycle club and dated frequently. His adoptive mother was forced to work and she was known for keeping Bianchi home from school for extended periods of time.

While in high school, Bianchi set high standards for his many girlfriends such as complete fidelity and outwardly absolute devotion; however, these standard did not apply to him.

He graduated in 1971 from Gates-Chili High School in Rochester and, soon after, married his high school sweetheart, Brenda Beck; however, the couple divorced after only eight months. Rumor has it that Brenda left without a word.

Bianchi enrolled at Monroe Community College to study police science and psychology after deciding that he wanted to become a police officer; however, after only one term he dropped out and then was rejected for several positions both in Rochester and, later, Los Angeles. Consequently, Bianchi worked a series of menial odd jobs, eventually becoming a jewelry store security guard for which he was fired for stealing and giving his girlfriends the stolen jewelry. He would steal from other employers over the years.

He then left Rochester and moved to Los Angeles in late 1975 at the age of 26.

Angelo Buono, Jr.

Angelo Anthony Buono, Jr. was born on 5 October 1934, also in Rochester, New York, to first-generation Italian-American immigrants originally from San Buono, Italy. His parents divorced when he was young and a five-year-old Buono moved to Glendale, California, with his mother Jenny and his sister Cecilia, where his mother supported the family by doing piecework in a shoe factory. Raised Catholic, this had no effect on Buono's development as a decent human being.

Buono displayed a very high interest in sex from a young age and when he was a teenager claimed that he had raped and sodomized number of girls. Buono idealized serial rapist Caryl Chessman, also known as "The Red Light Bandit", calling Chessman his hero but added that Chessman should have murdered his victims. He developed a deep loathing of women and desire to injure and humiliate them, including his mother who he would verbally abuse; however, he was emotionally tied to her until her death in 1978.

Buono began stealing cars and was sent to the Paso Robles School for Boys.

In 1955, Buono married his high-school sweetheart, Geraldine Vinal, who was 17 years old at the time, who he had impregnated; however, less than a week later he left her. She would later give birth to a son, Michael Lee Buono, on 10 January 1956. Buono filed for divorce and refused to pay child support or let his son call him "Dad". He was back in jail for car theft when his first son was born.

Later, he impregnated Mary Castillo who gave birth to his second son, Angelo Anthony Buono III, at the end of 1956 and then married her in 1957. The couple would have four more children: Peter in 1957, Danny in 1958, Louis in 1960, and Grace in 1962. In 1964, Buono was believed to have sexually assaulted his two-year-old daughter Grace; however, there is insufficient literature to know fully the circumstances of the allegation. Buono's second marriage to Castillo also ended in divorce that same year after she purported that he had been physically, emotionally, and sexually abusive toward her. In a last-ditch effort to reconcile with him, Castillo was "rewarded" with his handcuffing her and threatening to kill her at gunpoint. Castillo would later recount a night during the first year they were together where Buono tied her spread-eagled to the bedposts and "raped her so violently she was afraid that he was going to kill her" and "her pain seemed to him his greatest pleasure" and, thus, he had no qualms of hurting her and didn't seem to care that the children witnessed the abuse. He avoided paying child support again.

Buono married a third time in 1965 to a 25-year-old single mother named Nannette Campino and the couple had two children of their own: Tony in 1967 and Sam in 1969. Despite being treated as poorly as Mary Castillo had been, Campino feared for her life on a daily basis but stayed until he began to sexually abuse her 14-year-old daughter. Buono allegedly bragged that he raped his stepdaughter because "[s]he needs breaking in" and then turned her over to his sons for their pleasure. Campino finally took her children, filed for divorce, and fled the state in 1971.

Buono, again, was arrested for auto theft and was sentenced to one year in prison; however, due to his large family his sentence was suspended so he could work to support them.

Buono married yet again, on a whim, to a woman named Deborah Taylor; however, the couple did not live together, nor did they ever divorce.

In 1975, he became a car upholsterer and purchased his own place at 703 E. Colorado Street to live and work. Despite his abuse, cockiness, overbearing nature, and lack of good looks, Buono was considered very attractive by women, particularly younger ones who were usually naïve about sex so it was easy to convince them that his outrageous demands and proclivities were normal. Thus, he frequently forced women to engage in sex acts with him and began a relationship with a teenage girl whom he twice impregnated.

He was ugly inside and out; very coarse, vulgar, ignorant, selfish, and sadistic.

Bianchi and Buono Together

At the age of 41, Buono came into contact with his cousin Kenneth Bianchi, the latter who, in 1975, moved to California and in with his cousin. Bianchi found his older cousin with "dyed black hair, gold chains around his neck, a large gaudy turquoise ring on his finger, red silk underwear and a virtual harem of jailbait girls". Buono taught Bianchi how to use fake police badges in order to coerce free sex from prostitutes. When they needed money the two also became pimps for a short time until the two girls who worked for them—Sabra Hannan and Becky Spears—escaped after enduring relentless abuse by Buono. Bianchi, still desiring to become a police officer, applied for jobs at the Los Angeles Sheriff's and Glendale Police Departments but neither were hiring. He then procured employment with a title company and used his first paycheck on an apartment and a Cadillac, moving in with coworker Kelli Boyd. Boyd rejected his marriage proposal as she considered Bianchi to be very jealous, immature, and a liar; however, in May 1977 she told him she was expecting their first child together. The couple moved to an apartment at 1950 Tamarind Avenue in Hollywood.

Bianchi also rented some office space and set himself up as a psychologist with a fake degree and credentials. He did not have many clients and when Boyd found out she was outraged. During the "Hillside Strangler" investigation, Bianchi told Boyd he had lung cancer and was undergoing chemotherapy and radiation to explain for his work absences; however, this was a lie. One day, detectives came to his apartment to ask questions but were "favorably impressed" and did not consider him a suspect at that time.

The Murders

In October 1977, the two men committed their first murder together. Their M.O. was to cruise around Los Angeles and use fake badges to convince women that they were undercover police officers. After persuading them into Buono's car that the men said was an unmarked police car, the two would take their victims to Buono's house where they would rape, torture, and strangle them with their "signature" weapon—a garrote (a handheld ligature such as a chain, rope, or strap)—although some of their victims were reportedly killed by lethal injection, electric shock, and gas asphyxiation. Their bodies were thus disposed of outside, frequently in hilly areas.

Yolanda Washington, 19

19-year-old tall, leggy, African-American prostitute Yolanda Washington disappeared on 17 October 1977 from Cathedral City, California. She was found the next day dumped just outside Forest Lawn Cemetery, beaten, raped, and strangled with a piece of cloth. Her corpse was cleaned and there were faint marks around her wrists, ankles, and neck. Her body was posed in a grotesque sexual position.

Judith Lynn Miller, 15

On 31 October, 15-year-old Judith Lynn Miller, a runaway, was found in a La Crescenta-Montrose neighborhood, face up on a parkway in a residential area. The homeowner covered her with a tarp so that neighborhood children wouldn't see her. After the incident, that same homeowner relocated his family to another state.

The victim was small and thin, perhaps 90 pounds, with medium length reddish-brown hair. She had bruising around her neck. She had also been raped and sodomized and her body had been posed with her legs in a diamond-like position.

Los Angeles Sheriff's Department Sergeant Frank Salerno was called to the site. He noticed insect activity upon her skin and on her eyelid was "a small piece of light-colored fluff" that he saved for forensic experts. He surmised that she had been killed elsewhere and her body had been deliberately placed where it would quickly be found.

At her autopsy, the coroner determined that she had been killed around midnight and was raped and sodomized.

There was no missing person's report matching this latest victim so after a couple of days, Salerno had the newspapers run a small story on her with a request to contact the police if anyone could identify her. Still nothing. Salerno then took her picture to Hollywood Boulevard and showed it to hundreds of runaways, addicts, homeless people, and prostitutes. The name Judy Miller kept coming up as a young destitute prostitute. One man named Markust Camden—a self-proclaimed bounty hunter—told Salerno that he saw Judy Miller leave the local fish and chips restaurant at 9:00 p.m. the night before she was found dead. In fact, he would pick Buono out of a police photo lineup, but failed to recognize Bianchi.

Eventually, Salerno was able to track down the Miller family and got a positive identification. They had nothing useful to contribute to the investigation.

Elissa "Lissa" Teresa Kastin, 21

Lissa Kastin, 21, was working as a waitress at the Healthfaire Restaurant to pay for ballet lessons as she was an avid dancer. She also worked part time for her father's real estate and construction business. She was last seen leaving work the night of 5 November. She was found the next day near the Chevy Chase Country Club in Glendale on 6 November; which was also near to where Buono lived. She had been beaten, raped, and strangled to death.

Salerno compared notes with the Glendale Police Department and noticed similarities between his latest victim and this new one. Both bodies had the same five-point ligature marks—ankles, wrists, and neck—and had been dumped within six miles of each other. This latest victim had been raped but there was no evidence of sodomy.

When Salerno looked at the dump site he was confident that at least two men were involved due to the large guardrail between the street and where the body was found and the near impossibility that one man could have gotten her body over it alone.

Dolores Cepeda, 12 and Sonja Johnson, 14

After their early murders failed to attract much publicity, Bianchi and Buono decided to find some younger victims.

12-year-old Dolores Cepeda and 14-year-old Sonja Johnson were abducted in Highland Park, California, on 13 November.

They had last been seen getting off a school bus heading home from St. Ignatius School and approaching a large two-tone sedan that, reportedly, had two men inside.

Both young girls were found on 20 November in the hills between Glendale and Eagle Rock, near Dodger Stadium by a young nine-year-old boy who was treasure hunting in the trash on the hillside.

Los Angeles Police Department Homicide Detective Dudley Varney had been called to this site.

Kristina Weckler, 20

That same day, 20-year-old Kristina Weckler was found on the other side of the same hillside where Cepeda and Johnson were found.

Weckler was a quiet, loving, and serious honors student at the Pasadena Art Center of Design and lived in Glendale.

She was found nude, raped, tortured, and strangled to death as evidenced by ligature marks on her neck, as well as around her wrists and ankles. She had blood oozing from her rectum and bruises on her breasts. Weckler was the first victim to show additional overt signs of torture; having been injected with Windex glass cleaner she had oozing injection marks on her arms.

Los Angeles Police Department Homicide Detective Sergeant Bob Grogan—Varney's partner—was called to this site. He noticed that there was no indication of any disturbance of the foliage in the area or evidence that the body had been dragged there. Grogan made a mental note that she likely had been killed elsewhere and then carried and dumped in this location by one or maybe two men.

At this point, police were entertaining the idea that there was more than one killer and that they were becoming increasingly more sadistic.

Jane Evelyn King, 28

28-year-old actress Jane King disappeared in Los Angeles around 10 November 1977, and was found near the Los Feliz off ramp of the Golden State Freeway on 23 November. She had been sodomized and strangled and her body was badly decomposed. After King was found, Los Angeles Police Department officials—in addition to Glendale Police Department and Los Angeles County Sheriff's Department officers—created a task force to catch the "Hillside Strangler".

Lauren Rae Wagner, 18

18-year-old student Lauren Wagner lived with her parents in the San Fernando Valley. Her parents had gone to bed on 28 November, expecting their daughter to return home before midnight. The next morning, they found her car parked across the street with the door ajar.

Wagner was found later that day in a wooded area near Glendale's Mount Washington area. She was lying partially in the street, nude, with ligature marks on her ankles, wrists, and neck. Wagner, too, had been tortured as the palms of her hands contained several burn marks.

At the dump site was also a "shiny track of some sticky liquid, which had attracted a convoy of ants". Police considered that if the substance was saliva or semen from the killer then, perhaps, his blood type could be determined, as tests on semen found inside the earlier victims revealed nothing. It was later found that Bianchi was not a secretor, in that his blood type could not be determined by other bodily fluids. DNA testing had not come into popularity at this time.

When Wagner's father questioned the neighbors, it turned out that the woman who lived in the house where his daughter's car was parked, Beulah Stofer, saw Wagner's abduction. Stofer said that Wagner had pulled over to the curb at around 9:00 p.m. and two men had parked their car beside hers. After some type of disagreement, Wagner "ended up in the car with the two men".

When Grogan went to talk to the neighbor, she told him that she had just had a phone call from a man with a New York accent who told her to "keep her mouth shut about what she had witnessed or he would kill her". Stofer also told Grogan that the car was a large dark sedan with a white top and that one of the men dragged Wagner from her car into his while Wagner protested, "You won't get away with this!" Stofer described one man as tall and young with acne scars while the other was older and shorter, Latin-looking, and with bushy hair. She said she was positive that she would identify them again. This statement rang true when she picked both Bianchi and Buono out of a photo lineup shown to her by Grogan.

Kimberly Diane Martin, 17

Tall, blonde prostitute Kimberly Martin, 17, disappeared from Echo Park, California, and was found strangled to death on 13 December 1977 on a steep hillside on Alvarado Street. Martin had worked for the Climax "modeling agency".

Police believed they had two reasonably good leads in this case. First, Martin's last "client" called her to 1950 Tamarind, apartment 114; however, this turned out to be a vacant apartment. Secondly, the murderer called from a payphone in the lobby of the Hollywood Public Library on Ivar Street. Unfortunately, nothing came from these leads.

Cindy Lee Hudspeth, 20

On 16 February 1978, 20-year-old Bible school teacher and secretary at an Echo Park church Cindy Hudspeth was found in the trunk of her bright orange 1977 Datsun B210 that had been pushed over a cliff on Angeles Crest in Los Angeles National Forest near La Canada. She had been raped and strangled, with the strangulation marks similar to those associated with the "Hillside Strangler".

Hudspeth was also a neighbor of Weckler even though the two women did not know each other. Interestingly, Bianchi also lived in the same apartment complex; however, this lead was never pursued even though both Grogan and Salerno believed that there was a good chance that at least one of the murderers lived in the Glendale area.

After this case, the lack of additional victims resulted in the disbanding of the "Hillside Strangler" Task Force.

Jill Barcomb, 18 (originally believed to be a Hillside Strangler victim)

18-year-old prostitute Jill Barcomb was abducted in Beverly Hills and found near the famous Hollywood sign on 9 November. Whereas it was originally believed that she was a victim of the "Hillside Strangler" because she had been raped, beaten, and strangled, in 2005, her death was conclusively proven through DNA analysis to have been committed by Rodney Alcala, the "Dating Game Killer".

Also, sometime in 1977, the two men gave Catharine Lorre a ride with the intent of killing her; however, when they learned that she was the daughter of famous actor Peter Lorre who played a child murderer in Fritz Lang's 1931 masterpiece film M, they let her go. She had no idea who the men were until they were arrested.

The two stopped killing after their ninth victim, Hudspeth (although at this time it was presumed they had ten victims with Barcomb), likely due to the birth of Bianchi's son and, as some surmise, that he had made some acquaintances within the Los Angeles Police Department who would take him on ride-alongs around the city, ironically, looking for the killers, and Bianchi could talk about nothing else while in police presence. On the night they had tried to abduct another victim, the two men got into a heated argument when Bianchi told his cousin that he had been questioned in the "Hillside Strangler" case. After Bianchi's confession about being questioned by police, Buono, furious, threatened to kill his cousin.

Bianchi's Washington Murders

Bianchi's girlfriend, Kelli Boyd gave birth to their son, Sean, in February 1978, and in March Boyd decided to return to her parents in Bellingham, Washington, as she was tired of both Los Angeles and Bianchi's lifestyle. After three months of pleading to be reunited, Boyd relented and Bianchi moved to Washington in May. Bianchi's role as boyfriend and father was relatively successful and he even took a job as a security guard, ultimately earning the trust of his supervisors. However, this way of life did little to alleviate Bianchi's murderous urges. Within six months he was actively looking for new victims.

On 11 January 1978, Bianchi lured two Western Washington University students—roommates Karen Mandic, 22, and Diane Wilder, 27—to a house he allegedly "guarded" under the pretense of housesitting. Once there, he raped, tortured, and murdered them.

On 12 January, police were informed that two female students were missing after Mandic's boss became worried that she didn't arrive at work that day. He did remember that she had told him she had accepted a housesitting job in a wealthy Bayside neighborhood from a security guard friend of hers. When former-priest-turned-Bellingham-Police-Chief Terry Mangan went to the girls' home he found a hungry cat, as well as the address of the home where they were to housesit. The name of one security guard kept coming up, as well as a record that Bianchi had used a company truck that same night, supposedly to take into the shop for repairs. This never happened. Mangan began to consider the fact that the women had met with foul play.

Police then went to the Bayside house and found a wet footprint. They also interviewed a neighbor who told them that a security guard asked her to check on the house except for the night the women disappeared because "there was special work being done to the alarm system and he didn't want her to be taken as an intruder".

After a press conference, a woman called police to report that a car had been abandoned near her home in a heavily-wooded area. In the car were the bodies of Mandic and Wilder. Both had bruising and had been strangled to death.

Mangan had the security guard picked up. He gave them no trouble. His name was Kenneth Bianchi.

There was ample forensic evidence in this case; most notably foreign pubic hairs on the girls and fibers from the house's carpet matching fibers on the dead girls' clothing and shoes. Additionally, when police searched Bianchi's home they found several items stolen from job sites where he worked.

Remembering back to the "Hillside Strangler" cases in Los Angeles—and knowing Bianchi had lived there—Mangan called the police departments in California who had worked on the task force. He spoke to Detective Frank Salerno to whom everything finally made sense. Detectives tirelessly worked to link Bianchi to the strangler cases and were confident that he was one of the murderers.

Investigation and Arrest

Bianchi was not as careful this time, having left significant clues, most notably his car with California license plates was seen and subsequently connected to the addresses of two Hillside Strangler victims. Without mastermind Buono, Bianchi didn't have the wherewithal to cover his tracks.

Bianchi was arrested the following day, on 12 January 1979.

Buono was arrested on 22 October 1979, after Bianchi told police about his cousin's complicity in the murders.

Trial and Conviction

Prior to his 1981 trial, Bianchi decided to plead not guilty by reason of insanity and claimed to have a separate personality named "Steve Walker" who had committed the murders. After several interviews by experts specializing in multiple personality disorder and hypnosis, it was determined that he was faking. Immediately after Dr. Martin Orne mentioned to Bianchi that in genuine cases of multiple personality disorder there are typically at least three personalities, Bianchi created another alter ego named "Billy", shortly followed by two more. It was later determined that the name "Steven Walker" came from a student whose identity Bianchi had previously tried to steal to enable him to fraudulently practice psychology. Further, in Bianchi's apartment investigators found several psychology books which laid credence to Bianchi's ability to fake the disorder. He was eventually diagnosed with antisocial personality disorder with sexual sadism.

During trial, there was significant physical trace evidence against the two men; including fibers from Buono's upholstery from his home and workshop on two of the victims; an imprint of a fake police badge on his wallet; and hairs from rabbits he had raised on another victim.

Bianchi agreed to plead guilty and testify against his cousin in order to get leniency, albeit uncooperatively (evidence of his passive-aggressive personality disorder).

Judge Ronald M. George—who would later become California Supreme Court Chief Justice—said during Buono's sentencing hearing, "I would not have the slightest reluctance to impose the death penalty in this case were it within my power to do so. Ironically, although these two defendants utilized almost every form of legalized execution against their victims, the defendants have escaped any form of capital punishment." On an interesting side note, George's roommate at the time was author Darcy O'Brien who, four years after the trial, wrote a book about the case.

Both men were sentenced to life in prison.

While incarcerated, Buono married mother-of-three Christine Kizuka in 1986 while she was visiting her husband—and father of her children—who was in the cell next door to Buono at the Los Angeles County Jail, serving 18 months for assault with a deadly weapon. She worked as a supervisor at the California State Employment Development Department.

Whereas the 64-year-old Bianchi continues to serve his life sentence at the Washington State Penitentiary in Walla Walla, Buono died of a heart attack on 21 September 2002 while serving life at Calipatria State Prison in Calipatria, California. Denied for parole on 18 August 2010, Bianchi will next be eligible for parole in 2025.

Aftermath

Bianchi is also a suspect in the "Alphabet Murders"—also known as the "Double Initial Murders"—which occurred in the early 1970s in his hometown of Rochester wherein three young girls were raped, strangled to death, and dumped in the wilderness. At the time he worked as an ice cream vendor situated near two of the murder sites. On 16 November 1971, ten-year-old Carmen Colon disappeared and was found two days later in Churchville, New York, 12 miles from where she was last seen. 11-year-old Wanda Walkowicz disappeared on 2 April 1973 and was found the next day in Webster, New York, off State Route 104, seven miles from Rochester. Finally, on 26 November 1973, Michelle Maenza, 11, disappeared and was found two days later in Macedon, New York, a mere 15 miles from Rochester. They were called the "Alphabet Murders" because not only did the young victims have the same initial for their first and last name but they were also found in cities which began with the same letter.

Whereas Bianchi has repeatedly tried to get his name cleared from these murders he remains a suspect because his vehicle was seen near two of the murder sites.

Another series of murders with similar circumstances occurred in California in the late 1970s and investigators have hypothesized that they are connected to the Rochester "Alphabet Murders". In 1977, Roxene Roggasch, Paula Parsons, and Carmen Colon (like one of the original "Alphabet Murder" victims) were found raped and dead. Whereas Bianchi was tried for six murders, DNA exonerated him of the California "Alphabet Murders".

A 2008 movie entitled The Alphabet Killer was very loosely based upon the murders, and in 2010 a book written by Cheri Farnsworth called Alphabet Killer: The True Story of the Double Initial Murders was released.

In 1980, Bianchi started a relationship with a Veronica Lynn Compton, who was a defense witness during his trial. Compton, a cocaine addict who was fascinated by serial killers, was working as a scriptwriter in Hollywood. On one of her numerous visits with Bianchi while he was incarcerated, she gave him a copy of her screenplay entitled The Mutilated Cutter, about a female serial killer, and asked for this input. Compton grew increasingly fixated and allegedly fell in love with Bianchi. Later, she was convicted and incarcerated for attempting to strangle a cocktail waitress who she had lured to a hotel in a ploy to have the world—and authorities—believe that the real "Hillside Strangler" was still on the loose and that the wrong man was incarcerated. To make it look like an authentic "Hillside Strangler" murder, Bianchi manipulated and used Compton as a means to get out of prison by giving her semen of his smuggled out of the facility in a rubber glove to plant on the body. Despite that DNA forensics had not been utilized at that time, semen could still be analyzed to demonstrate the killer's blood type; however, Bianchi was not a secretor. The intended victim managed to get away and Compton was tried and convicted of first-degree attempted murder and sentenced to life. Compton was paroled from prison in 2003.

In 1992, Bianchi sued Catherine Yronwode for $8.5 million for putting an image of his face on a trading card. He claimed his face was his trademark. The case was dismissed with the judge saying that if Bianchi's face was, indeed, his trademark during the murders then he would not have tried to hide it from police.

In 2007, Buono's grandson, Christopher Buono, shot his grandmother—Mary Castillo who was married to Buono at one time—and then committed suicide. Christopher was unaware of his grandfather's true identity until 2005.

Bianchi and Buono are immortalized in film. The 1989 film The Case of the Hillside Stranglers—based on O'Brien's book—starred Dennis Farina as Buono and Billy Zane as Bianchi. In the 2004 film The Hillside Strangler, Buono was portrayed by actor Nicholas Turturro and Bianchi was portrayed by C. Thomas Howell.

The 2006 movie Rampage: The Hillside Strangler Murders starred Tomas Arana as Buono and Clifton Collins, Jr. as Bianchi.

In 2001 the Discovery Channel aired an episode of The New Detectives that revisited the murders.

Bianchi and Buono have also been mentioned several times on the television show Criminal Minds as an example of killer teams with psychopathic predatory sexual sadist personalities who murdered their victims together.

ROADSIDE STRANGLER

JASMINE GREY

When one envisions a serial killer, they think of a cold, calculating, heartless monster. As humans, some of us have developed ways to recognize other humans that are looking to cause us harm. If we look at a mug shot of famous another serial killer, like Charles Manson or Jeffery Dahmer, one could say that these men "look" like serial killers. Maybe it's because of their wild eyes, the way that they hold themselves, or the "creepy" feeling one receives from their presence. These factors are enough to make a person stay as far away from the killer as possible, but sadly, not all predators come with a warning sign. Michael Bruce Ross, later to be known as the Roadside Strangler, was a ruthless predator that slipped under the radars of the multiple women that he attacked, raped, and murdered. Detective Malchik, Ross' arresting officer, described this serial killer as, "There was nothing threatening about him, there was no signal to any of these people that there was a dark side or something that they should be afraid of. He was able to conceal that until it became time for him to attack these innocent, young women." Ross seemed to be an average-looking man of completely average-strength and abilities, but underneath his calm and normal exterior beat the heart of a man who struggled with his sadistic, sexual compulsions. When someone spoke to Michael Ross, they would say that he put off a very friendly and articulate demeanor seemed very well educated and kind, but it was merely a costume that he had created over a lifetime. The creepy part about Michael Ross, despite how honest and upfront he is about his murders, is the mystery behind his words. Is he being genuine or is this merely an act? Is he being honest or are we being deceived? His state of mind drifts from monotone claims to not possess any remorse for his monstrosities to genuine pleas for a chemical castration to reduce his perverse sexual desires. Michael Bruce Ross' case was a strange one, to say the least, and his mental condition will forever be remembered as a very dark part in Connecticut history.

The Childhood

Michael Bruce Ross was born on July 26, 1959. Among three other children, Michael Bruce Ross was born into the life of a middle-class chicken farmer. His mother Pat was impregnated in high school and forced into a shotgun marriage with Michael's father, Dan Ross. Needless to say, they did not go on to lead a very happy marriage. Pat Ross was a very mentally unstable woman, who underwent two abortions and was institutionalized twice. She abandoned her children and family once to run off with another man, but she soon returned to a depressing and emotionally unhealthy life on the farm. Pat Ross seemed to resent Michael more than the other children. His sister claimed that Michael received the brunt of their mother's aggression. Michael Ross claimed that he didn't remember his dark childhood or his emotional abuse-ridden family; he only had fond memories of working on his father's farm. The joyous memories of working on the farm centered on his peculiar job; Michael's job was to ring the necks of sick and malnourished chickens.

He recalled that he began to experience sexual fantasies around this time, like most boys his age, but they weren't anything like the hellish compulsions he faced in his adulthood. He explained his boyish daydreams as non-violent, although they might've been considered peculiar by most. In an interview, Michael describes his early, innocent fantasies of women, "I would kidnap women and take them to my safe place, and then they would fall in love with me, and never want to leave." It has been said that Michael was molested as a child by his mentally ill uncle while babysitting. As an adult, Michael Ross claimed that he did not remember this incident or his uncle at all; Michael was only six years old when the suspected uncle committed suicide. Whether Michael was too young to recall the incident or if he merely repressed the memory, the irreparable damage that comes along with molestation could be a very influential part of Michael's slip into sexual sadism. Despite his strange desires, his dysfunctional family, and his history of abuse, Michael was considered to be a pretty average child. As a teenager, he excelled in school, graduating as number sixteen in his high school class, and he eventually moved to Cornell University to study Agriculture and Life Sciences.

College Years

He continued to excel academically throughout his years at university. He studied Economics, Agriculture, and Life Sciences, and excelled in all of his academic endeavors. He joined the FFA (Future Farmers of America) and the Alpha Zeta fraternity. Ross' sophomore year roommate and Alpha Zeta brother, described Ross in 1977, "He kind of followed his own drum and went his own way." Michael never made any real connections in his fraternity, nor did he really make connections to anyone besides the long string of girls that he dated. In his college year, Michael Ross was rarely without a girlfriend, and he was rarely thinking about anything but. "There was always a certain obsession on his part regarding women," said his Alpha Zeta roommate, "That seemed to be such a big issue, a constant topic—needing a woman, needing to have a girlfriend. He would be obsessed about the relationship."

Ross claims that he did not experience truly violent sexual fantasies until his years at Cornell University. He especially did not begin to fantasize about raping women until his sophomore year in college. Michael Ross said that somewhere in his undergraduate years, he began to embrace the desires that brewed within him. He started his downward spiral with a very small step. He began to stalk his fellow students on campus. He would follow close by, making it known that he was behind her. "I would get a thrill by them knowing that I was following them. That they would be scared and that gave me a thrill," Michael explained his early experimentation with his predatory nature. When simply stalking the women wasn't enough, Michael eventually turned to towards rape. He hid in the bushes of Beebe Lake and raped a visiting student. Later, he attempted to rape another girl outside of the school observatory but failed. These assaults were only stepping stones to the full-fledged horror that Michael Ross was destined to cause. During his senior year at Cornell University, Michael Ross met Dzung Ngoc Tu, a Vietnamese student, and his very first murder victim.

The case of Dzung Ngoc Tu perplexed officials everywhere. She was found on May 17, 1981, in the Fall Creek Gorge. She died from a skull fracture and her body laid there for five days until she was discovered. It appeared to be a suicide, as if she had jumped from the bridge overhead and hit her head upon the fall, but there was no suicide note left at the scene. Close friends and family of Dzung Ngoc Tu claimed that there absolutely no signs of suicidal tendencies when she was alive and investigators found absolutely no reason for killing herself. Her body showed no signs of sexual abuse, there were no suspects, and the police had no idea that the culprit was actually Michael Ross, a man who was only connected to her by their similar majors. The case went cold when the police couldn't find a suspect. It wasn't until Michael Ross was already in prison for the murders and rapes of four other women when he confessed to murdering and raping a Vietnamese girl that went to his school in New York.

The Attacks and Murders of The Roadside Strangler

Michael Ross chose his victims merely off of chance and circumstance. If he encountered a woman that was in a vulnerable position, he felt this undeniable compulsion to attack. "There's nothing they could've said or done. It was me, it wasn't them," Michael Ross admitted with a solemn tone of voice, years after his final attack, "They were dead as soon as I saw them, I think."

Michael claimed that he only attacked women to relieve pressure that built up from his personal relationships with the women in his life. When he was working in North Carolina, shortly after he graduated from college, Michael recalled that he had a very difficult visit from his fiancé, which caused him to attack a random woman shortly after he dropped his fiancé off at the airport. He noticed a woman walking on the sidewalk with a baby stroller, so Michael pulled the car over and attacked her, using her own child as a weapon. "I told her that if she didn't do what I wanted, I would smash the baby's head against the wall of the house," Michael described in an interview, he seemed as if he were on the verge of tears, "I've always said that I never understood why these women never really resisted me. I'm not a big, strong guy, but nobody ever seemed to fight. I've always just contributed it as I must say something like that, or similar to it, to the other victims." He raped and strangled the woman, then left her for dead in her driveway.

On June 15, 1982, a 23-year-old woman named Debra Smith Taylor was attacked by Michael Ross in a park. He pulled her over where no one could see them, raped her, and forced her to roll over on her stomach; he then strangled her from behind. The young girl's body was discovered much later in a dried up river bed, only a few miles away from the location of another of Ross' victims, Tammy L. Williams. "Each time I killed, I made myself believe that I wasn't going to kill again," Michael Ross explained in an interview. It wasn't very long before he killed again.

His next attack occurred on a cold Thanksgiving Day in 1983. Michael Ross encountered Robin Stavinsky outside of Norwich State Hospital. He saw the woman in a vulnerable position and he took advantage of the situation. He forced the 19-year-old girl into a wooded area and demanded her to remove her clothing. Ross forced himself on the young girl then told her to roll over on her stomach. He strangled her from behind until the innocent Robin

Stavinksky died in his hands. "Serial killers like to strangle their victims and that is, I guess, the most common form of killing because there's more of a connection there. It's more real and it's not as quick," Michael Ross explained why he enjoyed strangling so much. After he was finished with her, he covered her body with leaves and left her for dead.

The Roadside Strangler struck again on Easter Sunday, 1984. April Brunias and Leslie Shelly were hitchhiking on the side of the road when Michael Ross happened to drive their way. He pulled over and offered the young girls a ride. The girls did not find Ross threatening so they got into his car and asked him to drop them off at the next gas station. When Michael passed the gas station, one of the girls drew a kitchen knife and threatened to stab him. In an interview Michael Ross explained what happened next, "I almost drove off of the road, I was so surprised. I don't know what I said, but I said something and she gave the knife to me. It obviously scared her." He parked the car at Beach Pond and used a cloth to bound both of the girls by their hands and feet. He put Leslie Shelly in the trunk of his car, then dragged the girl named April a few feet away from the car. He raped the young girl, flipped her over onto her stomach, and strangled her until she died. He then took Leslie out of the trunk and did the same thing to her. "The smallest one, Leslie Shelly, has always bothered me more than the others. I think it was because she was so small, I think it was because she was so cooperative, and I think it was because the way she was killed was so close to the fantasy. That was the one that was... it was like it was fantasy," Michael explained. The girls were only fourteen years old when they were murdered.

It was a summer afternoon, around three o'clock on June 13, 1984, when the Roadside Strangler committed the murder that would finally get him caught. He was driving home from work when he passed Wendy Baribeault, who was walking down the side of busy Route 12 in Libson, only a few miles away from his home. Michael Ross pulled the car over and began to speak to this 17-year-old girl; he repeatedly invited her to his company picnic. After a little bit of conversation, Michael forced the beautiful, young girl over a stone wall and into the woods. "When I attacked her, I don't believe that I was in control. I don't think I would've been able to stop," Michael Ross explained his mental state during this attack, "I didn't really feel anything. I knew what was going on and I saw what was going on, but it was more like watching an old film…" Michael then raped the innocent girl and strangled her, just like the others, then entombed her in the stone wall that lined the busy road. The road was so busy, in fact, that there were several eyewitnesses to the attack.

The Investigation of the Roadside Strangler

The police had absolutely no leads on the murderer (a.k.a. The Roadside Strangler) that had taken Connecticut by storm. That was until Wendy Baribeault's body was found. There were dozens of eye witnesses to her attack and composite drawings were created that matched the facial features of local Michael Bruce Ross. Witnesses also noted that the attacker was driving a blue Toyota. Michael Malchik, the investigator assigned to the case, compiled a list of several thousand blue Toyotas. This tiny bit of evidence eventually led investigators directly to Ross' house, which was only three miles away from the location of the crime scene. Michael allegedly dropped hints that he was the murderer upon speaking to the police. "It all had to end," Michael Ross explained. It wasn't long before Michael was called into an interview with police in 1984. After a few hours of grueling interrogation, Michael Bruce Ross confessed to all crimes that he'd committed in Connecticut, but left out the murders in New York. "It's a mystery to me to this day, but it's typical of him," stated Detective Malchik, "Here he is, confessing to six murders, and he thought enough ahead not to tell us about the New York ones. Looking back at it, it's obvious he was thinking of something. He was always thinking two steps ahead. He's got his own agenda, but I couldn't for the life of me tell you what it is."

When Michael confessed to the murders, he seemed very sorrowful and remorseful, but he claimed not to feel a blink of remorse, "I don't want to say that I don't have any remorse, it's just like they weren't real..." Michael explains his feelings towards hid victims in a later interview, "I can't see them as I was killing them, so when I say I don't have any remorse, that doesn't mean that I don't have any regrets, or wish that didn't happen, or there was something that I could do to bring them back or anything – I don't have any feelings towards them. I feel like I should be tormented by them - by what they look like when I was killing them – or tormented by what was happening immediately before I killed them – but none of that's there. None of that's there at all."

"The only time he said he was sorry, was that he was sorry for getting caught," Michael's arresting officer explained, "He (Michael Ross) told me matter-of-factly, he said, 'If you hadn't caught me, I would've just kept on killing, again.'" This eerie statement by itself was enough to put the Roadside Strangler to death immediately, but his strange nature kept investigators questioning his motives behind being so upfront and honest about his heinous crimes. Did he secretly want to get caught? Was this all part of some big plot to instill his insanity?

Anne Cournoyer, Michael's correction counselor, described his mannerisms as he spoke of the horrible crimes that he committed, "One minute he's very, you know, looks like he on the verge of crying, and the next minute he's sort of giggling nervously - or sadistically – you just really don't know. You think that maybe, it's out of nervousness, but he could be getting pleasure out of talking about it."

A full-scale investigation of Michael Bruce Ross' life led to the realization of his wavering mental stability. Michael Ross explained that he could never recall the faces of his victims, even directly after the murders, "You'd think that if you killed someone, you would have the face imprinted in your mind and that you wouldn't be able to get it out of your mind – I don't have that. I never had that," He explained, "The only faces I could see was what was in the newspapers a few days later when they were missing. You know, the high school pictures and 'anybody know where this girl is?' type of thing. When I think of them, that's the picture that I see. I don't see them as they were when I killed them. If you had stopped me right after and gave me a composite drawing of like twelve pictures - you know - some blondes, brunettes, whatever – I wouldn't have been able to pick them out. Even immediately after I killed them."

The names of all eight women were: Dzung Ngoc Tu (25), Paula Perrera (16), Tammy Williams (17), Debra Smith Taylor (23), Robin Stavinksy (19), April Brunias (14), Leslie Shelley (14), and Wendy Baribeault (17). He was only charged with the murders of the four Connecticut women because the murders of Dzung Ngoc Tu and Paula Perrera took place in New York. He was sentenced to death on July 6, 1987, but remained on death row for eighteen years after his sanity was called into question.

The Curious Case of Michael Bruce Ross

Michael spent the next eighteen years of his life caught in a battle of the Connecticut justice system. In court, a team of psychiatrists flocked to the defense of Mr. Michael Ross. After a parade of psychiatric evaluation, Michael was deemed mentally unwell, due to his dark childhood and his undeniable compulsions. Dr. Fred Berlin, the well-known co-founder of the Johns Hopkins Sexual Disorder Clinic, testified that Ross was struggling with a mental disorder called sexual sadism. Meaning that he gained sexual excitement from the pain and suffering of others. This discovery alone was not enough to save Ross' life, but Michael's claim to lose all self-control during the murders was enough to set back his execution date. Connecticut's state psychiatrist reluctantly agreed that Ross was not mentally capable enough to be responsible for his own actions, and therefore, it was not right to put him to death. Dr. Robert Miller wrote in a private letter, "I can't see how I could testify against psychopathology playing a sufficient role in defendant's behavior." Although this letter was never presented in court, Michael Ross' death sentence was overturned in 1994 and a new sentencing hearing was scheduled in 2000.

Michael Bruce Ross spent most of his time on death row writing about the mental disorder that took hold of his entire life. Michael claimed to have no control over his actions due to his compulsions. He described his sexual sadism as "a mental illness that drove me to rape and kill" and "made me physically unable to control my actions." During his time in prison, Michael still fell victim to his compulsions. It was impossible for him to control his sexual desires, so he spent the first few months of his incarceration reliving the murders. He claimed that he would fantasize these murders over and over again, hurting himself and causing sores from compulsive masturbation. It wasn't very long before he begged for some type of relief from his sexual desires, which came in the form of chemical castration. Ross was given medication that was designed to lower his testosterone levels and it finally relieved him from his sadistic compulsions. Thanks to this medication, Michael Bruce Ross was finally able to think clearly and he was able to see the true nature of his crimes.

The team of prosecutors naturally disagreed with the defense's attempts to lessen his blame. Prosecutors claimed that if he were unable to control his desires, he would've made less calculated attacks. It was reasonable to assume that Ross experienced these sexual desires constantly, which means that he probably experienced these feelings while in public places, or places where his actions could've been seen and reprimanded. Instead, Ross chose his victims very carefully, only acting when the girls were vulnerable and alone. Disproving the defenses' claims more so was the fact that Ross' hid their bodies after the attack, which further strengthened his blame and the case that he knew precisely what he was doing when he was doing it. "I'm not saying I wasn't there or it was multi-personality or any of that type of crap," Michael Ross later explained the strange fog he experienced while he murdered these innocent women, "I was there and I did it, but I wasn't one hundred percent there." To set light upon Mr. Michael Ross' guilt, Prosecutors relied on the "Policeman at the Elbow" test: would

Ross have committed the crime even if a policeman had been standing next to him?

The defense team immediately disagreed with the statement that all of Ross' attacks were calculated and well thought out, considering the murder of Ms. Wendy B. who was murdered next to a busy road with several eyewitnesses, "When I attacked her, I don't believe I was in control. I don't think I could've stopped." Michael spoke about the murder that eventually resulted in his incarnation. "Could he control himself? Well, two juries rejected that," Detective Malchik recalls, "As the state's attorney said at the trial if Ross was so out of control, why didn't he just rape the girl in between the yellow lines of Route 12? He made it simple for the juries to understand."

John Blume, a professor at the Law school and co-founder of the Cornell Death Penalty Project, noted the how the jury in Ross' case did not take the opinions of the psychological experts seriously. "The thing that's disturbing," Professor Blume stated, "is that even when the experts all say your client is insane, juries will still reject it." Despite the team of psychologists on Ross' side, claiming that he was completely unable to stop himself from committing these monstrosities, the jury chose not to believe them.

Somewhere in the eighteen years of Michael Ross' incarceration, he decided that he did not deserve to live anymore. Shortly after Michael wrote a story called "It's Time for Me to Die", he reconnected with a woman named Kathy Jaeger, who served as his pastoral advocate that converted Ross to Catholicism. Ross wrote in a newsletter that Jaeger, "was able to breach my defenses and was able to touch my soul as no one else ever has." He later called Ms. Kathy Jaeger "the most important woman in my life" and claimed that "If I were a free man, I would ask her to marry me." Although Kathy rejects his claims to romance, she continued to support Michael Ross throughout his decisions.

After she entered Michael's life, there was a great shift in the nature of his case. Michael was done fighting for his life and the mental condition that wreaked havoc on his entire existence. After his original death sentence was overturned in 1994, the court ordered a new penalty hearing, but instead of going through the hearing with his public defenders, Ross acted as his own attorney. He worked with prosecutor C. Robert Satti to created what was deemed as "death pact" that allowed the imposition of the death penalty without a penalty hearing. "Please allow me to go into the courtroom . . . to accept the death penalty as punishment for my actions," Ross wrote in a letter to Satti. "I'm not asking you to do this for me, but for the families involved, who do not deserve to suffer further and who, in some small way, might gain a sense of peace of mind by these actions and my execution." The "death pact" was rejected by the judge as a "short cut" involving a human life, so Michael Ross flip-flopped back into his old ways. Ross returned to his defense team and reverted back into fighting for his life, claiming that his crimes were merely a product of his mental illness. He was resentenced to death soon after.

Jaeger said that Ross's sudden acceptance of death was a sincere attempt to provide closure for the families of his victims, "He told me, 'You know I don't want to do this. But I have to.' He just really felt anguish over what he had done. Really, really harsh anguish and self-loathing. Contrary to media reports, he doesn't want to die. He wishes that the justice system got it right years ago and gave him life sentences because he does have a mental illness. And the sad thing is, if they had done that, the families of his victims wouldn't have been re-victimized [by the ongoing appeals]. Michael is trying, in essence, to save them from any more of that."

Whether his acceptance of the death sentence was sincere, or not, Michael Bruce Ross was sentenced to death by lethal injection on May 13, 2005. He chose not to speak any last words before his death and died peacefully in the execution chair. Some family members believed that his death was too peaceful. Debbie Dupuis, Robin Stavinsky's sister, stated that she thought she would "feel closure" but instead just "felt anger" as she watched Ross simply lay there, go to sleep and die.

The state of Connecticut finally decided to end the life of the Roadside Strangler and put an end to the anguish that the families had to endure. After a very tragic and dark lifetime, Michael Bruce Ross and his sadistic compulsions were finally laid to rest.

Conclusion

Michael Bruce Ross is the type of cold, calculating, manipulative killer that we only read about in horror novels. His crimes almost seem too heartless and brutal to be true, but the victims of the Roadside Strangler would tell you that he is nothing but a cruel reality. In only a few years, Michael assaulted a countless number of women and murdered eight. Although he was only charged with four murders, Ross was forced to withstand eighteen long years of debate over his life sentence. In prison, he transitioned from a vicious killer who was truly non-remorseful for his brutal crimes to a man who seemed to genuinely regret his life choices and the pain that he subjected. Towards the end of his life, Ross begged for removal from his troubled existence, not only for himself but to end the long and grueling process of the legal system. Despite his transition into humanity, Michael Bruce Ross never took full blame for his actions. He flip-flopped between blaming his childhood, his compulsions, and his interpersonal relationships for these terrible crimes. He claimed to never feel any guilt or remorse for his actions, simply because he wasn't completely there while they were taking place. During these attacks, Michael claims that he was under some type of spell, some type of fog that completely disconnected him from his actions. He was completely able to murder and rape these innocent women without feeling guilt or remorse, or even being able to recall the very faces of his victims', only moments after their attack. Michael Ross was an extremely troubled man who suffered from a very extreme case of sexual sadism. Michael explained his cruel, heartless, attacks with vivid details and an undetached tone of voice. The scariest part about his calm demeanor is the monotone way that he described the way he stole the lives of these young, innocent women. He speaks as if he were not responsible for killing these beautiful and young women, although he willingly confesses to the murders. He claimed that he was merely a victim of his sexual compulsions since his college years and the women he attacked were merely in the wrong place at the wrong time. Whether his desires were really uncontrollable or if it was merely an excuse, Michael Bruce Ross' case remains to be one of the most perplexing cases in American history. His mere mental condition was enough to perplex the entire state of Connecticut – how could this well-spoken, articulate man with such a great personality, commit these terrible crimes? Why didn't anyone notice his decline and stop it? What was it that made this seemingly normal man snap into the Roadside Strangler? Although the answers to these questions are uncertain, they definitely are unnerving. Michael Ross was created by circumstances, by his dark upbringing, and a lifetime of people letting him slip through the cracks. Everyone saw him as an average, everyday college student, so no one thought to ask. The woman that he murdered were sadly only stepping stones into the downward spiral into his sickness and they were eventually caused the end of his vicious, murderous cycle.

STOCKWELL STRANGLER : The True Story of Kenneth Erskine

62

NATALIE MARSHALL

Kenneth Erskine, known as "The Stockwell Strangler" due to the geographic proximities of his murders, was a deeply troubled young man who had demonstrated worrisome signs of violence and schizophrenia from a young age. He was a gerontophile in that he had an unnatural sexual attraction to the elderly. Gerontophilia, essentially, is the opposite of pedophilia. Erskine would break into elderly men's and women's London flats and strangle them while they were in bed; after which he would rape and/or sodomize most of them. To demonstrate his own warped sense of love for his victims he would cross their arms across their chest, close their eyes, and tuck them into bed. Also, perhaps to hide his shame, he would turn his victims' family photographs face down. There was much speculation among mental health professionals that Erskine also suffered from schizophrenia from a very young age.

He was eventually convicted of seven murders and one attempted murder and sentenced to life in prison in 1988 at the age of 25. However, in July 2009, following an appeal his murder convictions were reduced to manslaughter on the grounds of diminished capacity and he received a hospital order to serve his life sentences at Broadmoor Hospital. While he has the potential to be granted parole in 2028, the trial judge's original order was that Erskine should spend at least 40 years behind bars, thus making him at least 65 years of age before potential eligibility for release.

Early Life

Kenneth Erskine was born in Hammersmith, London in July 1963. His mother Margaret was British and his father Charles was from Antigua. He was one of four boys, had an average IQ when tested at eight years old, and was remembered by neighbors to be a "chubby, Bible reading soul"; however, he became increasingly violent and difficult to control. For example, as a child, Erskine had tried to hang his younger brother, John, twice.

Erskine was then sent to a series of schools for maladjusted and troubled children where he received his formal education. He frequently and violently attacked his teachers and classmates and was identified as inhabiting a fantasy world with murderous impulses. In his own private fantasy world he would take on the role of Lawrence of Arabia, attacking and tying up smaller and weaker children—a theme that would resurface when he targeted the weaker elderly during his murder spree. During a school-sponsored swimming outing he had attempted to drown several classmates by holding their heads under the water until teachers were forced to intervene. He set fires at school and once pushed a classmate off of a moving bus. On another occasion he stabbed a teacher in the hand with a pair of scissors. In another event, a psychiatric nurse who tried to examine Erskine was taken hostage by him as he held a pair of scissors to her throat. He strangled the classroom guinea pig. Whenever any female staff tried to be empathetic and show him any type of affection he would expose his genitals or rub up against them.

There was frequent talk that Erskine demonstrated clear signs and symptoms of schizophrenia as a teenager but nothing ever came out of it. He never had therapy or medication or any real psychiatric evaluation.

By the time Erskine was 16 years of age he had turned to drugs and particularly enjoyed inhalants. This latest display of misbehavior was too much for his mother who eventually kicked him out of the house, forcing him to survive on his own. When Erskine tried to give his younger brother marijuana she finally disowned him. He never saw any of his family members ever again and was forced to spend the next seven years of his life "drifting through the twilight world of London's homeless and rootless" living in squats and hostels in Brixton and Stockwell and getting involved with petty crime which primarily took the shape of failed burglaries on primarily the elderly.

Erskine's violent tendencies continued to worsen.

When he was 18 he stabbed a young male with whom he was having a homosexual relationship at the time. Erskine had burst into his boyfriend's bedroom and stabbed and slashed at his body while he lay in bed. Whereas this may have been the first attack of someone in bed it was a glaring omen of the terror he would wreak in six years.

Erskine was described my many who knew him as a persistent loner who drifted through life and due to no direction of any type of social support system started a life of crime. Erskine was also a Rastafarian due to his Caribbean heritage but was shunned by fellow Rastafarians due to his habit of theft.

An unsuccessful burglar, he was jailed on many occasions.

Among Erskine's favorite "drugs" were solvents—such as glue—which he would inhale. Among the most oft-cited short term effects of huffing glue are hallucinations, delusions, and hostility. Long-term effects include depression, irritability, memory impairment, diminished intelligence, and serious and sometimes irreversible brain damage. There continues to be speculation as to whether Erskine was born with his psychopathic tendencies (nature) or whether his upbringing and environmental stimuli were to blame for his problems (nurture). The consensus is that a combination of factors worked together to create Erskine's sick and murderous persona.

Erskine subsequently spent considerable time in Borstals—youth detention centers—due to being apprehended following his many failed burglaries. While in one for burglary in 1982 Erskine would paint and draw pictures of elderly people in bed with gags in their mouths, with daggers in them, or burned to death. Additional pieces of "artwork" included headless figures with blood spurting out from their necks, people holding human hearts in their hands, disemboweled people, screaming faces, and copious pools of blood. Again, this was a chilling omen of what was to come. In one documentary about Kenneth Erskine and his crimes, one of his cellmates at Borstal, named James, described how horrific Erskine's paintings were and how he would frequently smile and laugh while painting them. As Erskine's only "friend" James became his confidant as well. The two would play chess to pass the time and then there were Erskine's disturbing paintings. James stated in an interview that Erskine always spoke very quietly—rarely above a whisper—and was very weird.

Borstal doctors were concerned enough to the point of asking the authorities not to ever free Erskine because they were seriously worried that he might try to replicate his paintings; however, he was, in fact, released and four years later he would begin his killing spree.

The Crimes

At some point Erskine decided to act out his fantasies and began to murder. He is classified as a geographically-stable serial killer who confined his murders to a specific area. As Erskine had no vehicle and roamed around the Stockwell area frequently confining his murders to this area was likely due to simple necessity.

The Stockwell section of South London is a favored place for the elderly to retire. In the summer of 1986, however, a serial killer conducted a reign of terror throughout the community that resulted in seven known deaths—and possibly another four—attributable to The Stockwell Strangler.

Eileen Nancy Emms, 78

Emms was a 78-year-old retired schoolteacher who lived in an "unkempt basement flat" on West Hill Road in Wandsworth. She was sexually assaulted and strangled by Erskine on 6 April 1986.

Emms' body was found on 9 April 1987 by her home help who, upon knocking on her bedroom door and receiving no response one morning, let herself in to find Emms in bed with the covers pulled up to her chin, seemingly asleep. There were no obvious marks upon her body. Initially, the cause of death was attributed to natural causes. The doctor called to the scene estimated that she died approximately three days earlier and signed a death certificate that stated natural causes.

Once the victim's home help noticed that her small portable television was missing, the police were called.

During her autopsy, the medical examiner revealed that Emms had been strangled by bare hands. There was heavy bruising to her chest which strongly suggested that her assailant had kneeled atop her while strangling her. Further examination revealed that she had been sodomized as the assailant had left semen around her anus.

A short Afro-Caribbean head hair was found on her sheet.

Janet Crockett, 67

Janet Crockett was Erskine's first July 1987 victim. She was chairwoman of her local tenant's association. Her body was found on 9 June in her flat in the Overton Estate in Stockwell. She had been strangled but, unlike Erskine's first victim—and subsequent ones—she was not sexually assaulted.

Police were able to immediately conclude that she had been murdered as she had considerable bruising on her chest due to sustaining two broken ribs as a result of someone kneeling on her while she was strangled to death. Additionally, her nightgown had been ripped from her body and folded neatly and placed upon a bedside chair.

Police also noticed that framed family photographs on the bedroom mantel had been placed face down or turned around. This action would be repeated at several of his crime scenes and speculation abounds as to what Erskine's underlying motive for doing this was. Some psychological experts have surmised that his anger at his own parents' rejection without a healthy outlet for his emotions led to an insane jealousy of normal family ties. Another hypothesis was that he felt ashamed at his actions and didn't want any "witnesses."

Police were able to find a smudged thumbprint on a displaced planter and a palm print on the bathroom window.

Pathologist Dr. Iain West conducted Crockett's autopsy and compared it to Emms. He concluded that their methods of strangulation were similar. He stated that with weaker elderly victims unconsciousness would occur within 30 second and death after approximately three minutes. While Crockett's and Emms' murders were similar—and that they were both elderly—police had nothing else to link the two victims.

Frederick Prentice, 73

In the early hours of 27 June, 73-year-old retired engineer Frederick Prentice was asleep in his council-run elderly people's home on Cedars Road in Clapham when he was awakened by the sounds of someone entering his bedroom. He saw a young man enter and Prentice turned on his bedside lamp and ordered the intruder to leave. Erskine then pounced atop the old man, placed his index finger to his own mouth as a threat for Prentice to be quiet, and then sat upon his chest where he alternated squeezing his windpipe powerfully, then relaxing his grip, and repeated this multiple times. Prentice told police that his assailant had whispered only one word over and over: "Kill." Prentice was able to push the alarm button near his bed which caused his assailant to leave.

After talking to Prentice the police were fairly confident that all of the victims thus far were, in fact, linked. A shoeprint found at the scene would also serve to connect this attack with some of the other murders.

Prentice would later identify Erskine in a lineup.

Valentine Gleim, 84, and Zbigniew Stabrawa, 94

The next day Erskine murdered 84-year-old World War II veteran Valentine Gleim and 94-year-old Polish immigrant Zbigniew Stabrawa in their adjoining rooms at Somerville Hastings House, an old folks' home on Stockwell Park Crescent. Both men had been manually strangled and sodomized.

The intruder had been seen by alert night duty staff but had vanished before the police arrived. Point of entry was, again, determined to be an open window. Staff were also able to see Erskine fleeing the scene and estimated his height at approximately five-feet-eight-inches with a slim frame so at least now investigators had a clue about their suspect.

Of particular concern in these two cases was the discovery of a used flannel towel and electric shaver which suggested that the murderer had calmly washed up and shaved after killing two people.

Approximately one hour prior to the double homicide an elderly woman in a Stockwell old folks' home was attacked while she was in bed by a man grabbing her arm. She fought off her assailant so vehemently that he had to run off. Her description of Erskine matched Prentice's.

William Carmen, 82

Two weeks after his previous double homicide, Erskine struck again by strangling and sexually assaulting 82-year-old widower William Carmen on 8 July. This time he threw a monkey wrench at detectives by murdering on the other side of the Thames river, in Islington, North London. Carmen was discovered dead in his bed in his flat on the Marques Estate by his daughter. As was the case with Erskine's other victims, Carmen was in bed with the covers pulled up neatly to his chin and had been sodomized.

This time there was clear evidence of ransacking and theft as approximately £400 of Carmen's savings was missing. Family photos were also placed face down or turned around.

William Downes, 74

On 20 July the body of 74-year-old William Downes was found by his son in his Holles House on Overton Road flat in Brixton; the same location where Erskine's second victim, Crockett, lived. He was naked and in bed with the covers pulled up to his chin, his eyes closed, and his arms folded across his chest—classic Erskine signature. Downes' son had reminded him to keep his windows locked firmly at night a few days ago so as not to fall victim to the Strangler but he failed to heed these instructions and point of entry was, again, determined to be through an unlocked window.

Downes had been strangled and sexually assaulted like the majority of Erskine's other victims. There were semen stains on the sheets.

Investigators lifted a palm print from the kitchen wall and another from the garden gate which were eventually matched to the prints found at Crockett's home. Finding the owner of these prints, however, was not as easy as the process is today. In 1986, while fingerprints were on file on computer discs at Scotland Yard, palm prints were not. Investigators had a stack of four million files; however, by concentrating on London-based burglars and petty thieves, they were able to compile a more workable load. They were subsequently able to match the prints to those Erskine, a small-time crook with an extensive rap sheet for burglary.

Unfortunately, the police did not know where to find Erskine and while they were looking he struck again, killing his final victim.

Florence Tisdall, 80

80-year-old partially blind and deaf Florence Tisdall was found in her apartment at Ranelagh Gardens near Putney Bridge on 24 July. The caretaker of the apartments noticed her walker in the communal corridor and knew something was wrong as Tisdall was unable to get around without it. He found her strangled, sexually assaulted, and with broken ribs as a result of her killer sitting atop her chest. She had spent the previous day watching the televised wedding of the Duke and Duchess of York—Prince Andrew and Sarah Ferguson—even having her own hair done especially for the big event. Tisdall had lived in an almost empty block of flats where she had resided for the past 60 years. A cat lady, she had left her windows open so the cats could come and go as they pleased and this is how Erskine got into her flat.

It was at this scene where Erskine made, perhaps, his biggest mistake. Detectives knew immediately that Tisdall had been murdered because she was found in her nightgown, tucked into bed with the covers up by her chin. In reality, however, Tisdall's neighbors who frequently checked on her because of her disabilities stated that she always slept atop the covers in the clothing she had been wearing that day. When Erskine undressed Tisdall to rape her, he attempted to cover up his misdeeds by making it look as though she went to bed as usual and died of natural causes. Family photos were also placed face down or turned around as was the case at the Crockett crime scene.

One of Tisdall's neighbors stated that she saw Erskine near the victim's flat shortly after the murder had occurred "looking disgusted with himself." Thinking this to be odd she promptly notified the police.

All of Erskine's victims were pensioners and in all but one case there was evidence of sexual assault that took the form of sodomy; however, investigators and forensic specialists cannot say whether it occurred before or after the victims' death.

Investigation and Arrest

After the Crockett murder, Scotland Yard's Serious Crimes Squad Detective Chief Superintendent Ken Thompson—a Scotsman with 26 years' experience—was put in charge of the case and given over 200 detectives to devote to the search for The Stockwell Strangler. Interestingly, Erskine was originally nicknamed "The Heatwave Killer" because the murders occurred during the summer; however, when the majority of his murders occurred in and around Stockwell this nickname was changed. Further, plainclothes officers would stand guard throughout the night wherever the elderly lived.

At the height of the investigation, as many as 350 law enforcement officers were on the Strangler case which included 150 detectives and senior officers from the C1 Murder Squad who worked out of five separate incident rooms throughout London which were linked to a special Home Office computer. This network was called HOLMUS and was used to prevent wasting time by cross checking paperwork which proved to be detrimental to the investigation for Peter Sutcliff, The Yorkshire Ripper. Other police officers set up fixed observation points in neighborhoods with a high population of elderly residents and instituted extra patrols.

A psychologist was enlisted to create a profile of the Strangler and to provide potential insight into his signature to determine whether he was attempting to cover his tracks or was fulfilling some bizarre fantasy. The suspect was determined to be suffering from gerontophilia; or a sexual attraction to the elderly and the complete opposite of its better known opposite, pedophilia. Speculation abounded as to whether the killer's sexual paraphilia was a result of some relationship problems with his grandparents. Additionally, as his victims were all selected at random, authorities could not link the victims together with the hopes of finding some commonality between them that would enable them to identify and apprehend the man responsible.

The suspect was classified as a process-focused serial killer. The majority of serial killers are of this type; the other being act-focused wherein their own psychological gratification from the kill itself is the underlying cause. Instead, process-focused killers achieve a hedonistic psychological "reward." These types frequently "get off" on the method of their kill and they enjoy the perverse sexual thrill that accompanies the act of killing. The literature identifies four types of process-focused serial killers: gain in which the killer kills for profit or personal gain; thrill in which the act of killing gives the killer a rush or a high; power in which the killer enjoys dominating and manipulating victims and while sex is usually involved it is primarily tertiary to the kill itself; and lust wherein murder is associated with sexual pleasure and this type of killer will commonly have sex while in the process or killing or may engage in necrophilia after death. As far as Erskine is concerned, he can be classified in multiple subtypes. First, since he did rob his victims and steal money he demonstrates some elements of the gain process-focused serial killer. Secondly, he did obtain a rush or high from killing his victims and, therefore, does demonstrate some elements of a thrill killer. This element is particularly salient when he was seen by a witness—who would later testify against him—getting sick on the sidewalk after his final kill near where his last victim was found. The act of his getting sick appears to be directly attributed to the thrill her received from killing and having sex with his victim. Finally, since Erskine likely sodomized his victims after he killed them his sexual fantasies were of a higher priority than is typically the case for power killers. Thus, he demonstrates elements more aligned with a lust killer.

Coupled with the fact that Erskine targeted the same type of people and that he engaged in specific rituals which were part of his signature makes Erskine a classic serial killer. His smaller size likely contributed to his choice of the elderly as his victims because in their weakened conditions he wouldn't have much trouble overpowering them.

The palm prints were the most damning evidence investigators had at that point; however, they only placed Erskine at two of the murder scenes. Despite similarities among all of the victims' crime scenes, the fact that Erskine wasn't cooperating with police required detectives to find other evidence. Investigators from Scotland Yard took the unusual step of distributing his Erskine's picture to the media to try to find more witnesses and potential leads by hopefully jog people's memories as to whether anyone may remember seeing him. Thompson also did something very uncommon; he appeared on television, appealing to Erskine to turn himself in.

After Tisdall's death the search for Erskine intensified even more than was already the case; however, being that he was a drifter with no permanent address or any real belongings to speak of they had to search through the hundreds of hostels and squats in South London. His life was so devoid of meaning and friends to help detectives find him.

Investigators got their big break when they realized that since the suspect was likely unemployed that he would be receiving social security and unemployment benefits. Upon further investigation they discovered that Erskine picked up his benefits on alternating Mondays from a Department of Health and Social Security office in Southwark, South London, and that he was due to collect his next check on 28 July. The building was placed under surveillance and when Erskine turned up, right on time, he was arrested and handcuffed without any struggle.

Whereas items and cash from the victims' homes were, in fact, missing, police did not believe that robbery was the driving motive in the homicides. There were neither signs of struggle nor any signs of forced entry. Police surmised that Erskine entered the flats through unsecured windows.

Forensic evidence linking the cases relied upon the fact that the victims were all murdered in similar ways: by the assailant kneeling on the victims' chests and then placing his left hand over their mouths and strangling them with his right hand. The semen collected at nearly all crime scenes suggested the same genetic fingerprint in that the same suspect was responsible for all of the sexual assaults. Additionally, there was a single hair found in Emms' flat, as well as matching shoeprints from three of the scenes.

A hairdresser informed investigators that Erskine had approached her wanting his head and pubic hair bleached. While she agreed to the former she refused the latter. Apparently, while he was sitting in the shop waiting for the bleach to take effect he self-applied the bleach to his pubic region and eyebrows, the latter resulting in his getting chemicals in his eyes and requiring assistance in washing it out.

When questioned by Detective Inspector Brian Jackson and other detectives, Erskine's responses indicated that the detectives' jobs were to be much more difficult than they thought. Erskine spent the majority of the interrogation giggling, staring out of the window or into the sky, or masturbating. After he was arrested, psychologists placed Erskine's mental age at 11 even though he was 24 at the time. He had first denied that he was, indeed, The Stockwell Strangler claiming instead to be a petty burglar who had no motive to kill anyone. After vehemently denying his culpability and blameworthiness in the string of murders and seeing that he wasn't getting anywhere, Erskine then changed his tune and said, "I don't remember killing anyone. I could have done it without knowing it. I am not sure if I did it." He also tried to blame the murders on a whispering female voice in his head. He once stated,

"It tries to think for me. It says it will kill me if it gets me," and, "It blanks things from my mind."

He was clearly disturbed but not a fool in any sense. In fact, when searched, detectives found ten bank and building society accounts that Erskine had opened to hide the proceeds of his crimes. During the three-month span of murders, he had deposited over £3,000; quite a large sum of money for someone who was unemployed. This included a £350 deposit into one of his accounts on the morning after the Carmen murder. It was evident at this point that Erskine was amassing profits from his burglaries while simultaneously collecting unemployment benefits. This demonstrated that whereas Erskine did suffer from some degree of mental retardation and likely some psychosexual paraphilia he was not stupid by any means. In fact, he told detectives that his motive was to achieve notoriety. He said, "I wanted to be famous … I thought I would never get caught."

During a lineup—or identity parade as it is called in England—surviving victim Frederick Prentice was able to definitively identify Erskine. Another woman who had witnessed Erskine vomiting on the sidewalk near Putney Bridge a mere 200 yards from the scene of the final murder on the night in question also picked Erskine out of a lineup.

Trial and Conviction

Erskine's trial commenced at the Old Bailey on 12 January 1988. He pled not guilty to the charges of seven murders and the attempted murder of Prentice. During his trial he would stare out the window or down at his feet as was the case when he was interrogated. When details of the murders were brought up, Erskine would masturbate.

The jury heard him confess to the burglaries of the deceased victims; however, he claimed that someone else must have followed him and killed the individuals after he had left. Nobody was buying this story.

After an 18-day trial, the jury unanimously found him guilty on all eight counts and he was sentenced to seven life terms plus 12 years for attempted murder with a recommended minimum of 40 years; one of the heaviest penalties ever handed out in British legal history. However, diagnosis of schizophrenia and other mental illnesses pursuant to the Mental Health Act of 1983 led to a successful appeal of Erskine's murder charges which were eventually reduced to manslaughter. He is currently serving his time at the Broadmoor Hospital.

In addition to his seven known victims, the police suspected Erskine of four other murders for which he has never been charged due to insufficient evidence to prove that he was, in fact, the murderer.

John Jordan, 57

On 4 February 1986, 57-year-old John Jordan was found in his Josephine Avenue flat in Brixton strangled beside his bed.

Charles Quarrell, 73

73-year-old Charles Quarrell was found suffocated in his bed on King James Street in Suffolk on 6 May. He had two handkerchiefs stuffed into the back of his throat, effectively blocking his windpipe.

Wilfred Parkes, 70

70-year-old Wilfred Parkes was found on 28 May in his Stockwell flat, suffocated and in bed. A nearby pillow was presumed to have been the murder weapon.

Trevor Thomas, 75

On 12 July 75-year-old Trevor Thomas was found dead in the bath at his home on Barton Court, Clapham. As Thomas had been dead for quite a while there was inadequate forensic evidence for investigators to link his murder to the others; thus resulting in Erskine not being charged with his death even though Thomas was almost certainly one of his victims.

As mentioned, Erskine has never been charged with these additional deaths; however, police were so confident that Erskine murdered them that they effectively closed the book on all of these cases. There is also much speculation that he likely killed prior to his first known victim—such as was the case with Mr. Jordan—and that because of his choice of victims their deaths may have simply been attributed to natural causes.

Aftermath

There is not much more information on Erskine due to a lack of any detailed studies of him as is commonly the case with other serial killers where the literature is rife with speculation as to what influences led to the individual turning to serial murder. His only possessions were meager clothes and some books from the building society. Other than a post-arrest diagnosis of schizophrenia, the mind of Kenneth Erskine remains mostly shrouded in mystery. In fact, his mentally-disturbed state has worsened to the point where he has been told that he will never be released from Broadmoor Hospital.

Psychiatrists have never been able to fully penetrate his mind and discover what makes him tick. He clearly has a problem differentiating fantasy from reality and appears to be locked in his own childlike world. However, there is one incident that clearly demonstrates his understanding between right and wrong. On 23 February 1996, Erskine prevented the possible murder of Peter Sutcliffe, known as the "Yorkshire Ripper" by alerting guards while another inmate, Paul Wilson, attempted to strangle Sutcliffe with the flexible cord from a pair of stereo headphones. Erskine was able to restrain Wilson from inflicting further injury upon Sutcliffe until guards arrived.

Erskine found himself on the receiving end of an assault. On Christmas Eve in 1997 he was attacked by fellow inmate, 34-year-old Keith Hanger. Hanger was serving time for the 1992 shooting of his friend after having escaped from prison. He walked up to Erskine and squirted liquid from an aerosol can into his face before lighting it with a lighter. Erskine was taken to Frimley Park Hospital in Surrey, in agonizing pain and worried that he would lose his eyesight; however, his temporary blindness was just that—temporary.

Psychiatrists continue to attempt to probe Erskine's mind trying to uncover more and more of his psyche toward, perhaps, finding what makes him tick. Currently, he is unable to answer for his crimes, as demonstrated by the reduced sentence due to diminished capacity.

THE BOSTON STRANGLER

NATALIE MORTON

Albert DeSalvo, the infamous "Boston Strangler" is considered to be "America's first 'serial killer' of the modern era". He is responsible for as many as 13 women's murders in the Boston area between 14 June 1962 and 4 January 1964. Victims were as young as 19 and as old as 85. Whereas police did not believe that all of the murders were committed by the same person, the public was convinced that one person, dubbed "The Boston Strangler", was the sole suspect.

During the hunt for the Boston Strangler, police were also investigating two separate strings of rapes committed by the "Measuring Man" and, later, the "Green Man"; both of whom were, in fact, DeSalvo. He was arrested on 27 October 1964. At the time DeSalvo was not connected to the murders; however, likely due to his insatiable thirst for infamy and attention, he confessed that he was. He was sentenced to life in prison in January 1967, and was stabbed to death while in prison in November 1973.

There continue to be doubts as to whether DeSalvo was truly the Boston Strangler. In 2001, DNA evidence proved that the semen left in his last victim's body was not DeSalvo's. Thus, the cases of the Boston Strangler—as well as why DeSalvo was murdered and who committed it—continue to remain open.

Early Life

Albert Henry DeSalvo was born on 3 September 1931—the third of six children—in the poor town of Chelsea, Massachusetts, to Frank and Charlotte DeSalvo. The DeSalvo children, particularly Albert, had miserable childhoods. Frank was a violent alcoholic who would bring prostitutes home and have sex with them in front of his wife and children. On one occasion Frank broke his wife's fingers, one by one, by bending them backward and knocked out all of her teeth. Frank was also physically abusive with his children and allegedly once sold young Albert and two of his sisters as slaves to a farmer who paid $9.00 for all three of them.

The details of the following six months are unclear as DeSalvo never talked about it.

Not having any healthy relationship upon which to use as a model, DeSalvo desperately sought the love of women. He claims that he and his siblings experimented with sex acts as young as five years old and that he started having sex at age eight with girls and women, in addition to prostituting himself to homosexuals. During his adolescence, DeSalvo was exposed to graphic sexuality; from his father's activities with prostitutes to his neighbors who were very promiscuous and who DeSalvo watched whenever he could and this likely had a huge impact on his sexual development and resulting paraphilia.

DeSalvo started school at age six and due to several childhood illnesses missed much school which resulted in his failing second grade and being placed into special education classes when he was in fifth grade. He graduated junior high school at age 16 and that was the end of his formal education.

As a child, DeSalvo tortured animals—one of the triad factors common to serial killers and present in 36% of serial murderers in an FBI study—and as a young adolescent he committed shoplifting and thefts, common to 81% of serial killers in the same study. As a result, DeSalvo had many run-ins with the law.

He began working at the age of 12; performing odd jobs such as delivering flowers and shining shoes in an effort to make life easier for his siblings who he loved very much. In fact, despite the violence and brutality for which he would be later known, he was very docile with his family members; even when provoked.

At age 16 he worked in a Cape Cod motel as a dishwasher and, in his free time, would watch couples making out through windows. His first sexual aberration was as a voyeur.

At this time, on 12 November 1943, DeSalvo was arrested for the first time; for battery and robbery of a newspaper boy—over

$2.85. He did receive a suspended sentence from incarceration but was sent to the Lyman School for Boys the following month. His IQ was tested while there and was 93; low-average. He commented after his arrest that one "can learn about every form of sexual perversion" in reform school. After his parole in October 1944, he obtained employment as a delivery boy; however, in August 1946 he was returned to the Lyman School for stealing a car.

When he was released the second time, at the age of 17 and with nothing more than a junior high school diploma, DeSalvo joined the Army and worked as a military police officer. During his time in the military he had a reputation for being obsessively clean and a self-proclaimed ladies' man who bragged about his many affairs with officers' wives. While he was getting the sex he craved, he said he didn't have the love he also wanted. In Germany DeSalvo met and fell in love with a young woman named Irmgard and they married in 1949.

Irmgard often complained that her husband's libido was too high and she did not want to have sex with him as often as he wanted it. She was also distressed by DeSalvo's common practice of masturbating frequently, sometimes even after they had just had intimate relations. His sexual problems would increase when he, Irmgard, and their infant daughter—Judy, born in 1955—returned to the United States after DeSalvo was honorably discharged from the Army in 1956. Judy had been born with a congenital pelvic disorder that caused a deformity in her legs which kept them in a permanent frog-like position so she required special braces. DeSalvo would massage her little legs and would tie bows around her braces.

The family settled in Fort Dix, New Jersey, where, less than one year later, on 5 January 1955, he was accused of molesting a nine-year-old girl while her mother ran out for a quick grocery trip. DeSalvo was apprehended and charged with carnal abuse of a child and released on $1,000 bail; however all charges were dropped when the mother did not want to subject her young daughter to having to testify in court.

The family moved to Boston to get a fresh start. DeSalvo took whatever jobs he could find; at a shoe factory, a shipyard, and then settled into construction work.

In 1959, the DeSalvos had a son, Michael.

DeSalvo was very restless working odd jobs but his lack of experience or education precluded him from finding anything he would consider to be better. DeSalvo always had a lust for infamy and he was already headed down that pathway.

The "Measuring Man" and "Green Man" Rapes

DeSalvo's "career" as a sexual predator began in 1961 when he pretended to be a representative of a black-and-white modeling agency and approached young women telling them that he had to take their measurements to see if they would fit the clothing. He would tell them that he was authorized to give them each $10 for taking measurements; $15 for doing so with the women clad only in a bra and panties, and $25 if they were nude, which would facilitate his sweet-talking himself into their beds for sex. However, some women complained to the police of his unwelcomed and inappropriate touching.

At this time, DeSalvo was also perfecting his breaking and entering techniques and was arrested for burglary; however, much like his earlier crimes, he managed to receive suspended sentences. However, DeSalvo made a serious misstep when, on 16 March 1961, he was arrested for burglary and, in an effort to self-aggrandize himself, told the police about his measuring "scheme". As would be expected, DeSalvo was promptly arrested for breaking and entering, assault and battery, and lewdness and was faced—for the first time in his life—with a prison sentence. In exchange for a guilty plea to the first two charges, the prosecutor agreed to drop the lewdness charges.

DeSalvo served 11 months in prison and was released in April, 1962. When asked why he perpetrated his "pathetic charade" DeSalvo said that he was neither good-looking nor educated but "was able to put something over on high-class people" and that he was able to outsmart college kids.

The first Boston Strangler murder would occur a mere two months later.

In May 1964, after the Strangler struck for the last time, there was another string of rapes in Boston, courtesy of DeSalvo. In this, his latest scheme, he was dubbed the "Green Man" because he would wear a workman's green overalls in order to gain access into single women's apartments under the guise that he was there to fix a leak or check something allegedly broken or whatever. Once inside, he would bind and sometimes rape the women. Occasionally he would ejaculate prematurely after he bound them and would then apologize and loosen their bindings. On some occasions he would also apologize to his victims when tying them up, telling them he had to fulfill "the urge." He never killed anyone during this time. Four victims went to the police and, as luck would have it, one police officer remembered DeSalvo from his "Measuring Man" assaults.

When the murders surfaced, the city of Boston's residents were terrified not simply because there was a serial killer on the loose but that the victims were not prostitutes or vagrants or some other type of "unsavory" character but respectable, middle-aged or elderly women who were attacked in their own homes. Things worsened when the murderer began targeting young women too.

The Murders

Initially, the Boston Strangler targeted elderly or middle-aged women; however, by December 1962, he had turned his attention to younger women with two victims being in their 20s.

While the manhunt for the Strangler was going on, Boston women were gripped by tremendous fear. Dogs were adopted from shelters in record numbers and hardware stores quickly sold out of deadbolt locks. Because there was never any indication of forced entry, police could tell women to be extra aware; however, the killings continued.

Anna Siesers, 55

In the evening of 14 June 1962, 55-year-old Latvian seamstress Anna Siesers was preparing a quick after-dinner bath before getting ready for her son, Juris, to pick her up for a church memorial service. The petite divorcee looked younger than her age would indicate and had left Latvia over a decade earlier with her son and daughter, relocating to the Black Bay area of Boston on 77 Gainsborough Street.

There was a knock at her door.

When her son arrived an hour later and could not get his mother to answer the door, he forced the door open and found her lying dead on the bathroom floor with the belt from her housecoat tied around her neck.

Boston Police officers James Mellon and John Driscoll found Siesers in a "shockingly exposed position": outstretched, on her back, her blue taffeta housecoat completely open, in a grotesque position with her legs spread apart. Her head was a few feet from the open bathroom door and the cord from her housecoat knotted tightly around her neck with the ends tied into a bow. This bow would become a signature of the Boston Strangler and some speculate that it had something to do with the bows DeSalvo would tie on his daughter's leg braces. There were also signs that Siesers was sexually assaulted with some unknown object.

The murderer made it look as though he ransacked her apartment; however, nothing of value was taken.

At first, police believed that the crime likely began as a burglary and when he saw the victim in her housecoat he couldn't control himself, sexually assaulted her, and then killed her so he couldn't be identified.

This first murder was highly organized and proficient. DeSalvo confessed that he parked his car blocks away, wore gloves, disposed of his bloodied clothing quickly, and engaged in conversation with someone on the street as an alibi.

Mary Mullen, 85

On 28 June 1962, DeSalvo knocked on 85-year-old Mary Mullen's door under the guise that he was there to do some repairs on her apartment. Of particular interest was that most of his victims' apartments were of lower-rent and always in need of some type of repair so the residents had little reason to disbelieve anything that he told them.

'DeSalvo said that when she turned her back to him he put his arm around her neck and that she must have died quickly from a heart attack. He left her body on the sofa and investigators ruled her death as from natural causes until DeSalvo confessed to having a role in it years later.

Nina Nichols, 68

Just two days later on 30 June, at 1940 Commonwealth Avenue in Brighton, retired physiotherapist and widow Nina Nichols, 68, met her unfortunate fate at the hands of the Strangler. She was talking on the telephone to her sister when her door buzzer rang. Nichols told her sister—who also heard the buzzer—she would call her back soon but never did.

Like Siesers, Nichols' apartment had been ransacked but nothing was taken. She was found with her housecoat and slip pulled up to her waist and her legs were spread. Two of her own nylon stockings were tied tightly around her neck with the ends culminating in a bow. She had been sexually assaulted with a wine bottle and there was seminal fluid on her thighs.

Time of death was determined to be around 5:00 p.m.

Helen Blake, 65

That same day, 15 miles north of Boston in Lynn, Massachusetts, 65-year-old Helen Blake was strangled with one of her nylons and her bra had also been tied around her neck and fashioned into a bow.

She was discovered face-down on her bed, naked, with vaginal and anal lacerations but no sign of seminal fluid.

Nichols' apartment had been ransacked and nothing was taken except for the two diamond rings she had been wearing. The murderer had also unsuccessfully tried to open a metal strongbox and footlocker.

Ida Irga, 75

The next time the Strangler struck was nearly two months later on 21 August, with 75-year-old "shy and retiring widow" Ida Irga his latest victim. She was found dead two days later at her apartment at 7 Grove Avenue in Boston's West End. Up until-and including this time—there were no signs of forced entry, indicating that she had likely voluntarily let the murderer in.

Sergeant James McDonald described how he found Irga: on her back on the living room floor, clad in a light brown nightdress that was torn, thus exposing her body. A white pillowcase was knotted tightly around her neck and her legs were spread open with her feet propped upon individual chairs, facing the door so her displayed body was the first thing anyone saw when they entered her apartment. A bed pillow was placed under her buttocks. There was evidence of sexual assault but no spermatozoa were present.

The pillowcase had been tied so tightly that she had dried blood inside of her ears and around her mouth. This would be common with most of the Strangler's victims.

Jane Sullivan, 67

On 30 August, nurse Jane Sullivan, 67, was found, murdered, in her apartment at 435 Columbia Road in Dorchester. She had been dead approximately ten days before she was discovered.

Police found Sullivan "on her knees in her bathtub with her feet up over the back of the tub and head underneath the faucet." Her face was in about six inches of water and her bare buttocks were exposed. Her underwear was around her ankles and it was determined that she was killed in another room and then posed. She may have been sexually assaulted as there was a broom with bloodstains on its handle; however, her body was too badly decomposed that it could not be definitively determined whether she had been.

Again, there was neither sign of forcible entry nor was the apartment ransacked; however, Sullivan's purse was found open.

The city of Boston was gripped with fear and the Strangler wouldn't strike for three more months; thus, giving police the opportunity to investigate possible suspects.

Investigators claimed that the posing of the victims, the selection of apartments, and the use of household items with which to strangle the victims demonstrates a disorganized-personality serial killer; however, DeSalvo's ability to talk himself into his victims' apartments and his attention to not leave fingerprints by wearing gloves is characteristic of an organized-personality serial killer. Thus, DeSalvo was classified as the rare mixed-personality type of killer—one that was both organized and disorganized at the same time and a very difficult challenge for investigators. DeSalvo was about to make it even more perplexing for detectives.

Sophie Clark, 20

The next murder occurred on 5 December—DeSalvo's wedding anniversary—and it sent detectives reeling. After having strangled six women to death in two months, the Strangler stopped for four months. Some believe that his anniversary may have triggered him returning to action. Also troubling was that instead of being an older white woman, 20-year-old Sophie Clark—a popular student at the Carnegie Institute of Medical Technology—was a young, pretty black woman. Most sexual murderers do not cross racial lines, nor do they typically have victims of such diverse ages. This led to much speculation that there were two murderers at large in Boston at that time.

Clark was found by her two roommates with whom she shared an apartment at 315 Huntington Avenue; a few blocks from Anna Siesers' apartment. Clark had been writing a letter to her boyfriend when the Strangler struck.

Like the other victims, Clark was lying on the living room floor, nude with her legs spread wide apart, and three of her own nylon stockings knotted and tied tightly around her neck, along with her slip. Again, there was evidence of sexual assault; however, this time semen was found. There were signs that Clark struggled with her attacker and he had rummaged through her magazines and record collection.

In his confession, DeSalvo said he talked his way into her apartment with his usual repairman ruse and then told her that he was scouting for models and he would give her $20-30 per hour. When he asked her to turn around, he grabbed her from behind.

Clark's neighbor, Marcella Lulka told investigators that at approximately 2:20 p.m. that afternoon a man knocked on her door telling her that the super had sent him to talk to her about painting her apartment. After telling her that he would have to fix her bathroom ceiling, Lulka said that the man asked her if she had ever considered modeling because she had a nice figure. She put her finger to her lips and said that he became angry, almost as though he changed completely. When she informed him that her husband was asleep in the next room, she said that he said he had the wrong apartment and ran out.

She described him as between 25 and 30 years of age, of average height with honey-colored hair, and wearing a dark jacket and dark green pants. The super stated that he had not sent anyone to any of the units and this was approximately the time Clark was murdered.

Patricia Bissette, 23

The last of the Strangler's victims for the year was 23-year-old secretary Patricia Bissette who was murdered on New Year's Eve, three weeks after Sophie Clark. Bissette's boss went to her apartment that morning to pick her up for work but she did not answer her door. After he got to work and saw that she had never arrived, he went back to her place at 515 Park Drive in the Black Bay area; very close to where Anna Siesers and Sophie Clark lived. With the assistance of the building custodian, her boss climbed through a window.

Bissette was found face-up in bed with the covers pulled up to her chin. Underneath the covers, however, she had several stockings knotted and entwined with a blouse that was also knotted around her neck and tied in the signature Boston Strangler bow. There was evidence of recent sexual intercourse and some damage to her rectum. Of particular interest to investigators was that Bissette's legs were together and she had been covered which usually indicates guilt on the part of the perpetrator.

DeSalvo, in his confession, said, "She was so different. I didn't want to see her like that, naked and ... She talked to me like a man, she treated me like a man." He said that he knocked on her door pretending to be looking for one of her upstairs neighbors whose name he had gotten from the downstairs mailboxes and she invited him inside to wait. She made coffee and they talked. He said that he didn't want to hurt her.

Bissette was in the early stages of pregnancy when she was killed.

Mary Brown, 69

On 9 March 1963, in Lawrence, Massachusetts—25 miles north of Boston—69-year-old Mary Brown was found beaten, raped, stabbed, and strangled to death after letting the murderer in believing he was there to fix her stove.

This time the murderer brought along a lead pipe which he used to bludgeon Brown about her head. He also stabbed a fork into her breast several times, leaving it embedded in her flesh. And also rather disturbingly, the assailant raped the victim after she was dead.

Beverly Samans, 23

On 6 May, pretty 23-year-old graduate student Beverly Samans missed choir practice at the Second Unitarian Church in Back Bay. A friend went to her apartment and unlocked her door with the spare key she had given him. The first thing he noticed was Samans lying on a sofa bed, her legs spread apart. Her hands were bound behind her back with one of her scarves and a stocking and two handkerchiefs were knotted together and tied around her neck. A cloth was places over her mouth that covered another cloth that had been stuffed into her mouth.

At first glance she appeared to have been strangled to death; however, the real cause of death was the four stab wounds to her throat. She had sustained an additional 18 stab wounds arranged in a bullseye pattern around her left breast. The ligature around her neck was not tied tightly enough to kill her. She had also been repeatedly raped. The bloody knife was found in her kitchen sink.

Her time of death was estimated at approximately 48 to 72 hours previously.

Because Samans was studying to be an opera singer there was speculation that her throat muscles were too developed and caused problems for the murder when he attempted to strangle her, thus resulting in his stabbing her to death.

Evelyn Corbin, 58

On 8 September, pretty 58-year-old divorcee Evelyn Corbin was found murdered in her apartment. She was lying face-up across the bed, nude, with her underwear stuffed into her mouth as a makeshift gag. It was determined that Corbin had been manually strangled and the killer left his trademark bow tied by a nylon around her ankle. There were several lipstick-marked tissues which contained trace amounts of seminal fluid. Spermatozoa were found in her mouth only.

Her apartment had been searched but nothing had been taken. Of particular interest was a lone, fresh doughnut outside her window on the fire escape that had not been put there by anyone in the building.

Joann Graff, 23

On 23 November 1963—the day after John F. Kennedy was assassinated and the entire nation was mourning his death—23-year-old conservative and religious industrial designer Joann Graff was raped and murdered in her ransacked Lawrence apartment by the Strangler. She had been strangled with two of her own nylon stockings which were tied tightly and in an elaborate bow around her neck. She had teeth marks on her breast and the outside of her vagina was lacerated and bloody.

The neighbor in an apartment in the building said he saw a young man in his mid- to late-20s with "pomaded hair" and dressed in dark green pants with a dark shirt and jacket knocking on the door of the unit across the corridor. The neighbor said that the stranger asked him if "Joan Graff" (mispronouncing her name) lived there. The neighbor told the man that she lived in the apartment below and then said that he heard the door below being opened and shut.

Ten minutes later, a friend tried to call Graff but there was no answer.

Mary Sullivan, 19

Sullivan would be the Strangler's last victim and also his most brutal murder. On 4 January 1964, she was found by her roommates atop her bed, naked, and propped against her headboard with her legs wide open, knees bent, and a broomstick handle inserted into her vagina. There was seminal fluid dripping from her mouth onto her breast and also seminal stains on the blanket. She had been manually strangled and a stocking and two print silk scarves were tied around her neck into a large bow. A cheery Happy New Year card was left by her body.

After this last Boston Strangler murder was committed, DeSalvo began another string of rapes; the "Green Man" ones.

Investigation and Arrest

Almost immediately after Sullivan's murder, Massachusetts Attorney General Edward Brooke took over the investigation and on 17 January 1964 he announced that the Boston Strangler cases was his top priority. Brooke created the Strangler Bureau that was headed by Assistant Attorney General John S. Bottomly; this choice much to the chagrin of Boston Police Commissioner Edmund McNamara. The team was comprised of Boston Police Detective Phillip Di Natale and Special Officer James Mellon, Metropolitan Police Officer Stephen Delaney, and State Police Detective Lieutenant Andrew Tuney.

A medical-psychiatric advisory committee was also created and headed by Dr. Donald Kenefick. The latter's first priority was to develop a criminal profile. They decided that the Strangler was at least 30 years old; neat, orderly, and punctual; works with his hands or has a hobby involving handiwork; probably single or divorced; would not come across as crazy to the casual observer; and has no close friends of either sex.

Several so-called experts had and continue to have conflicted opinions as to whether DeSalvo was, in fact, the Boston Strangler.

DeSalvo was arrested on 3 November 1964 after a "Green Man" victim identified him—the police remembered DeSalvo from his "Measuring Man" cases—and he was taken to the Bridgewater Mental Hospital.

Strangely, his wife was not surprised as she knew her husband was obsessed with sex and that one woman would never be enough for him. In fact, the "Green Man" assaulted four women in one day in different cities in Connecticut. He admitted to breaking into roughly 400 apartments and assaulting some 300 women; however, DeSalvo's propensity for exaggeration left investigators doubting as to whether this was an accurate number.

DeSalvo confessed to 13 murders as the Boston Strangler—two more than the police thought.

At Bridgewater, DeSalvo struck up a friendship with convicted murderer George Nassar who would play a pivotal role in this case. DeSalvo allegedly confessed to Nassar who is also among the suspects in the Strangler case. Nassar has been serving a life sentence for the 1967 shooting death of a gas station attendant in Andover, Massachusetts. His multiple attempts for appeal have been denied by the Massachusetts Supreme Court in 2008 and 2009, as well as his 2011 request for a writ of certiorari by the United States Supreme Court.

Former prison psychologist Dr. Ames Robey, who examined both DeSalvo and Nassar, called Nassar a "misogynistic, psychopathic killer and a far more likely suspect than DeSalvo" as the Boston Strangler, and he is not the only one with this opinion.

Some speculate that since DeSalvo was going to serve life in prison for his role in the "Green Man" attacks, the two colluded so Nassar could collect the reward money that the two men would split. Further, some speculate that DeSalvo's tremendous need for notoriety made him believe that his confession would make him world-famous and that he might get book and movie deals from his "story".

During a 1999 interview, however, Nassar denied his involvements in the Strangler murders and that the speculation had "killed his chances for parole".

It was Nassar, in fact, who brought F. Lee Bailey and DeSalvo together as Bailey was also Nassar's attorney.

At one point in his confession, DeSalvo admitted, "I would go home and watch what I had done on TV. Then I would cry like a baby."

There was no physical evidence tying DeSalvo to the murders; however, he did know a lot of specific details. Something that disturbed the police was that DeSalvo's misinformation grossly matched the misinformation in the newspapers as well. Even family members of the Boston Strangler's victims believe DeSalvo was not the Strangler. They point to his taped confession and asserted that even though police said he had to be the killer because he knew things that only the killer would know, in fact, he confessed to certain events that simply did not happen. Therefore, many still believe—to this day—that DeSalvo got his information from the real Boston Strangler while in prison. Even DeSalvo's brother, Richard, believes that his brother confessed to being the Boston Strangler because he knew he was going to prison for life and wanted to "cash in" on book and movie deals while fulfilling his desire for fame, even if that fame was infamy.

Trial and Conviction

In an attempt to prove DeSalvo insane in his rape cases F. Lee Bailey tried to get his client's confession admitted into evidence; however, a restraining order and the appointment of a legal guardian for DeSalvo led to his confession being recorded but not used as evidence in his trial. Consequently, after an eight-day trial, the jury—after only four hours—found DeSalvo not insane and guilty of the "Green Man" assaults.

DeSalvo was sentenced to life in prison on 9 January 1967.

Escape and Death

In January 1967, DeSalvo and two other inmates escaped from Bridgewater Hospital. DeSalvo had left a note on his bunk addressed to the superintendent stating that he had escaped to force attention upon the hospital's conditions and to protest his being sentenced to a prison instead of a mental hospital. With the Boston Strangler loose again, the city was once again sent into panic.

Police offered a $5,000 reward leading to information on the whereabouts of DeSalvo and his own attorney, Bailey, offered to double that reward if his client was caught unharmed.

The first thing DeSalvo did was go see his brother Richard who gave him clothes and a gun. He then went to Lynn, Massachusetts, where the police department was already on alert. Dressed in an old Navy uniform, DeSalvo went into a shoe store and told an employee he needed to use their telephone because he "had to call F. Lee" who then called the police. One employee asked DeSalvo if he was the Boston Strangler, to which he replied, "I honestly don't know. I know I did some of them."

DeSalvo was rearrested in Lynn, Massachusetts, and was transferred to the maximum-security prison in Walpole where he later recanted his confessions.

On 25 November 1973, at the age of 42, Albert DeSalvo was stabbed to death in the Walpole Prison's infirmary.

Of particular interest was that DeSalvo called Dr. Robey a mere 12 hours before his death saying that he wanted to "tell the real story" of the Boston Strangler.

DeSalvo wrote a poem while incarcerated, a couple of years before he was killed. It ends:

Today he sits in a prison cell,

Deep inside only a secret he can tell.

People everywhere are still in doubt,

Is the Strangler in prison or roaming about?

Both DeSalvo's murder case and that of the Boston Strangler remain open; the latter due to doubts that DeSalvo was, in fact, the real killer.

Aftermath

In 2001, George Washington University Professor of Forensic Evidence James Starrs asserted that DNA evidence found on Mary Sullivan's body did not match DeSalvo's DNA. The team of forensic scientists revealed that their tests discovered DNA from two individuals other than Sullivan and that DeSalvo was not one of them.

Sullivan's nephew Casey Sherman, a television producer who penned a book in 2003 entitled A Rose for Mary, has spent the past dozen or so years trying to prove that DeSalvo did not murder his aunt based upon the fact that DeSalvo "was convicted solely on the basis of a confession, which was riddled with inaccuracies." Sherman, like others, believes that DeSalvo, being faced with many years in prison, made up his confession with the hopes of procuring a book and movie deal so he could support his wife and children. Further, Sherman believes that DeSalvo was killed in prison because he was preparing to tell the real story, that his death was a "hit", and that prison officials were complicit. Sherman alleges that in order to get to DeSalvo, his murderer "had to go through six checkpoints, stab him 28 times, and then go back through those six checkpoints covered in blood."

DeSalvo's life was the subject of the 1968 film The Boston Strangler that starred Tony Curtis as DeSalvo, Henry Fonda and George Kennedy as the officers who apprehended him; however, the film was highly fictionalized, assuming that DeSalvo was, in fact, guilty and suffered from multiple personality disorder. Additionally, the Rolling Stones' 1969 song, "Midnight Rambler" has lyrics based upon DeSalvo.

TIMOTHY WILSON SPENCER

JEFF THOMAS

Timothy Wilson Spencer has the distinction of being the first American serial killer to be convicted on the basis of DNA evidence—evidence that also exonerated a man who had been in prison after being wrongly convicted of committing one of Spencer's murders. A troubled adolescent from Arlington, Virginia, with a deep hatred of women, Spencer utilized his cat-burglar skills, strength, and agility to gain entry into his victims' homes, lay wait, and then bind, rape, torture, and murder them. In total, Spencer had been linked to five murders and at least nine rapes in both Richmond and Arlington, Virginia. He was convicted of the murders of four of his victims and sentenced to death. Spencer was ultimately executed in the electric chair on 27 April 1994.

Early Life

Timothy Wilson Spencer was born on 17 March 1962 in Arlington, Virginia, and raised in the Green Valley section of town which was known as a lower-income, tough, predominately Black neighborhood. His parents were hard workers and had attended college but had divorced when he and his younger brother Travis were young. Travis commented that their mom was the best mother ever who worked hard to support them and spent time with them.

As an adolescent he had become increasing rebellious, first getting into trouble at the age of nine and again at 12 for urinating and defecating in the school yard. He was a poor student but intelligent. In the professional literature Spencer would be classified as a life-course-persistent offender who began deviant behavior at a young age which continued throughout his life with escalating degrees of crime. He had been implicated and/or convicted of six prior burglaries (three as a juvenile) and three counts of trespassing before being arrested for burglary in 1984 for which he served three years in prison before being released to a halfway house in the Southside area that was a transitional residence for nonviolent offenders. Because Spencer's conviction was for burglary he was considered to be nonviolent even though the evidence would ultimately show that he was a deliberately violent rapist and murderer. While in the halfway house Spencer was a loner who ate at the end of the table away from others and even watched television away from the rest of the residents. He did speak to one woman who worked at the halfway house and worked on her car so that he could borrow it. Whereas among the house rules were that residents sign in and out every time they come and go and had to follow a curfew, this procedure was poorly supervised and enforced.

In an interview, Spencer's younger brother Travis reiterated his utter disbelief that his brother was capable of what he did. Burglaries and other property crimes he said he could accept but someone who displayed such anger toward and hatred of women and who wanted to control them as badly as Spencer did by the systematic torture and strangulation of his victims was too much for him to believe. He even mentioned one time in his childhood where he and a friend stole some candy from a local store and were brought home in a police car that his older brother told him to never become like him.

A big question that has remained since Spencer's execution was whether someone like him was the product of nature or nurture. Some forensic psychologists say that deviant sexual preferences are hard-wired and that when combined with certain other factors can lead to deviant and aggressive behavior. The literature suggests that predatory psychopaths suffer from atrophy of the parts of the brain responsible for moral decision-making and aggression control and whereas this may be genetically influenced, the right combination of such traits coupled with environmental influences can make someone commit heinous acts. Spencer exhibited some of the "classic" signs of the serial killer typology—bedwetting, cruelty to animals, and a propensity for setting fires—which facilitated the escalation of his actions from breaking and entering to arson to burglary to rape to murder.

The Crimes

Debbie Davis

Spencer's first reported victim was 35-year old Debbie Dudley Davis. On 18 September 1987 he entered her home through a kitchen window with a rocking chair below it and bound, raped, tortured, and murdered her. Detective Ray Williams—who was dispatched to this and each subsequent murder scene in Richmond and stated that he had never seen such disturbing crime scenes in his entire career—remarked that the intruder had to have been exceptionally strong and agile.

The assailant utilized materials found on the premises to fashion his homemade ratchet strangulation contraption and this would be a commonality at all his subsequent crime scenes. In this case, he utilized socks, shoelaces, and a 16-inch vacuum cleaner extension hose.

There was very little forensic evidence at the scene—no hair or fibers—and no witnesses which suggested that the assailant was very meticulous. Except for the semen.

Autopsy results on Davis suggested that she was murdered between 9:00 p.m. on Saturday, 18 September and 9:30 a.m. on Sunday, 19 September. At the time of her murder, Spencer lived 2.7 miles from her apartment which would be approximately a 37-minute walk. The halfway house log showed that he left at 7:30 p.m. on Friday and returned at 12:30 a.m. Saturday. Davis had spoken to her parents on the phone from 8:30 p.m. to 9:00 p.m. that Saturday evening.

She had been strangled with a sock and vacuum cleaner hose that the Virginia court said had been "fashioned into a ligature and ratchet-type device." According to the medical examiner, the contraption had been twisted two or three times, ultimately causing Davis' death. The pressure of the ligature was so strong, in fact, that her neck muscles, larynx, and voice box were cut; blood was congested within her head; one of her eyes suffered a hemorrhage; and her nose and mouth were bruised. Her hands were bound by shoelaces and were attached to the neck ligature. It was posited that the more the victim struggled, the tighter the ligature became and that the suspect did this repeated times before finally killing her.

There were copious amounts of seminal fluid at the scene on Davis' nightgown and sheets, and vaginal and anal swabs demonstrated the presence of spermatozoa. The amount of semen suggested that the perpetrator repeatedly masturbated while alternatingly tightening and releasing the pressure of the ligature on Davis' neck. Two foreign hairs were found in the victim's pubic hair that were later identified through forensic analysis as being Negroid and, subsequently, consistent with Spencer's underarm hair. With respect to the semen, investigators discovered that the suspect was a secretor, defined as someone whose blood characteristics are found in other bodily fluids such as seminal fluid.

Analysis of Spencer's blood revealed him to be a Type O, enzyme grouping PGM type 1, PGM subtype 1+, peptidase A type 1. This particular configuration is shared by 13 percent of the population; however, specific characteristics of the analyzed DNA demonstrated that the sample would match only one in 705 million Black individuals. There are only approximately ten million adult Black males in the United States.

Dr. Susan Hellams

Two weeks' after Davis' death, on 2 October Spencer struck again when he beat, raped, tortured, and killed Dr. Susan Hellams. Hellams' husband discovered his wife's beaten partially-naked body on the floor of their closet. Point of access was discovered to be a second-story window that had a large portion of screen cut from it. Detective Williams commented that this was one of the most brutal murders he had ever seen.

The medical examiner identified the cause of death as ligature strangulation from two belts around her neck. Hellams also sustained a fractured nose, blunt force injury to her lower lip, a number of bruises and scrapes, and an injury consistent with a shoe on the back of her leg. Petechiae in her eyes suggested that she had been strangled and revived for at least 20 minutes before she was killed which suggested that the assailant was likely aroused by having complete control over his victim, not unlike the Davis case. Evidence of rape and sodomy included seminal fluid on her back and in the gluteal fold; small mucosal tears of the anus; and the presence of spermatozoa on vaginal, rectal, and perianal swabs. Additionally, an ample amount of seminal fluid was found on the victim's skirt and slip. Subsequent forensic and serologic examination determined that the seminal fluid and spermatozoa were consistent with Spencer's secretion type and could not have belonged to Hellams' husband. DNA analysis ultimately proved that the fluids were Spencer's.

After Hellams' murder, the unknown perpetrator was dubbed the "Southside Strangler" and the area went into panic mode over the term "serial killer." Panic ensued in Richmond; residents of the area left their lights on all the time, every deadbolt lock was purchased from stores, and even dogs from local animal shelters were adopted in record amounts. Police had told single women to nail their windows shut. A preliminary profile suggested that he was a white adult male, approximately 35 years old, a loner, intelligent, not a criminal beginner, and likely had considerable success as a cat burglar of sorts due to his agility and ability to enter residences without making a sound.

The police sought to find a connection between the victims to help identify a suspect. Nearby Cloverfield Mall in Chesterfield County proved to be that link. Davis had worked in a bookstore and Hellams had purchased books from her.

Diane Cho

Not long after, on 22 November, 15-year old high school student Diane Cho was bound, raped, and strangled to death. Cho lived less than a mile from the Cloverfield Mall and wanted to go to medical school. She was studying in her bedroom when Spencer entered through her bedroom window and overtook her so quickly that her parents and brother who were in the next room didn't hear a thing the entire time Spencer was assaulting and murdering her.

Spencer had carved the infinity symbol on Cho which, according to experts, signified his taking, keeping, and sealing the victim for himself since she was a virgin.

Cho lived very close to the Cloverfield Mall.

Susan Tucker

While on furlough from the halfway house in Arlington visiting his family for Thanksgiving, Spencer attacked Susan Tucker, 44, in the same fashion as his other victims on or about 27 November (her body wasn't discovered until 1 December). She was home alone at the time as her husband was away on a business trip. Spencer entered through a basement window and Davis was hog-tied with a rope, raped, and subsequently died from ligature strangulation. When her body was found she had been dead for a few days and those on the scene remarked that it was extremely disturbing and unsettling.

During her autopsy four-to-eight intact non-motile sperm were collected from vaginal swabs and DNA from semen stains were determined to have been left by a secretor. As mentioned, Spencer was that secretor.

Carol Hamm

Back on 25 January 1984, 32-year-old attorney Carolyn Hamm was raped, bound, and hanged in the door between her garage and house. Her body was found naked, face down, and her robe was on the living room floor alongside a piece of cord cut from a Venetian blind and a knife.

At the time, a McDonald's janitor, David Vasquez, was arrested and convicted of Hamm's murder after two witnesses placed him on her street that day. Despite police having doubt that Vasquez was guilty because of his less-than-70 IQ, he did confess and was, subsequently, serving a 35-year prison sentence. Authorities wondered if he had a partner who might still be at large.

Absent any leads at the time, Detective Horgas visited Vasquez at the Buckingham Correctional Center near the Blue Ridge Mountains on 7 December 1988. Vasquez seemed confused; he retracted his confession insisting that he couldn't have killed Hamm because he didn't drive and had no way to get to her house after work. He also denied having an accomplice. After the interview Horgas told the warden that he believed Vasquez to be innocent.

Other Crimes

Prior to Hamm's murder, there was a string of rapes between June 1983 and January 1984 in Arlington. Nine women had been attacked by a masked Black male in his 20s who carried a knife and broke into their homes via a window and who was dubbed the "black masked rapist." The last rape, in fact, occurred on the day Hamm's body was discovered. Detective Horgas wondered whether these rapes and Hamm's murder were connected. When he heard about the first two murders in Richmond, Horgas called Detective Williams to discuss the similarities between Horgas' rapes and the Hamm murder in Arlington and the two (at that time) murders in Richmond. Williams also mentioned a recent attack in Davis' and Hellams' neighborhood wherein a Black masked man had entered a woman's apartment through a window and was in the process of tying her up when neighbors came over to investigate noises and scared him away. Whereas Horgas was virtually convinced that the crimes in both Arlington and Richmond had been committed by the same person, Williams was skeptical due to the distance between the two cities and the fact that FBI profilers asserted that serial killers are almost always White.

Williams did tell Horgas that the Richmond police were trying DNA testing which, he said, identified an individual's unique genetic material that is found in every cell of a person's body and that they had already sent samples from the Davis and Hellams murders to Lifecodes, a New York State private laboratory that analyzed DNA for paternity tests. Prior to this, nobody in the United States had ever used DNA testing in a homicide investigation.

The Investigation

All of the murders shared overwhelmingly similar characteristics which demonstrated that the deceased were the victim of a serial killer with a particular signature that was unique to him. All of the victims were bound—wrists to neck—with handmade tourniquets fashioned from materials the killer found at the house through which he could repeatedly tighten and loosen the ligatures so that he could suffocate and revive the victims multiple times. There was substantial semen left at the crime scene near the body which suggested that the suspect likely masturbated while torturing his victims. None of the victims had defensive injuries which demonstrated that they were overcome quickly. All of the victims were White or Asian with a "stocky" build. All of the murders occurred on the weekend. Additionally, in every case the victims' bodies were laid crosswise on their beds (except for Hellams who was in her closet) representing submissiveness and in each case the victims' were "covered": Davis was redressed in shorts, a sheet was placed over Cho's buttocks, a blanket was placed over Tucker's buttocks, and Hellams' closet door was closed. Some experts have suggested that posing the bodies enabled the perpetrator to extend the crime scenes to make him feel even more powerful than he already did and that his covering them was like putting a lid on a trash can. The point of entry in every case was through a window in which glass was either broken or a screen was cut.

Detective Horgas was the first to overcome what is known as "linkage blindness" in which clues exist to link particular crimes but the Richmond investigators wore blinders as to how certain cases were, in fact, linked. One of the most glaring examples of this was that Richmond police were so intent on looking for a White suspect based upon their preliminary profile and, therefore, were initially against considering the possibility that the killer was, in fact, Black.

Horgas also reinterviewed the burglary and rape victims from Arlington prior to Hamm's murder. He discovered glaring similarities and a pattern of escalation that ultimately culminated with the perpetrator "graduating" to murder. Similarities included the fact that the point of entry was always through a window; lengths of Venetian blind cords had been cut and found near the crime scenes in multiple cases; and victims had been tied up, raped, and tortured. In some cases the victims' mouths were covered with duct tape (Cho's mouth was also taped). The fifth victim was locked in a car that was lit on fire but she was able to kick her way out and escape. Perhaps most damning was that the three-year break in between Hamm's death and the other four women's deaths correlated to the time that Spencer was in prison and that for every recent murder he had signed out of the halfway house; even seeking approval for a furlough to return to Arlington for the Thanksgiving holiday.

And then there was the DNA evidence. In addition to the samples from Richmond, Horgas hand-delivered samples from the Hamm and Tucker murders as well as some of the rapes to Lifecodes on 28 December 1988.

While waiting for the results, on 29 December FBI agents Stephen Mardigan and Judson Ray from the Behavioral Science Unit at Quantico went to Arlington to examine Horgas' evidence and ultimately agreed with his theory that the crimes in both cities had been committed by the same person. The profilers said that the key to all of the crimes was to reexamine the first rape in Arlington and that the perpetrator likely lived nearby because he would have wanted to commit his first assault where he felt comfortable such as in his own neighborhood. The agents also iterated that based upon their profile, this type of person would only stop if he were incarcerated of died. This spurred Horgas to look for a suspect who was arrested and incarcerated shortly after Hamm's murder in January 1984 and released just prior to the first Richmond murder in September 1987.

Spencer demonstrated classic signatures of an anger-retaliatory rapist-murderer who utilized sexualized violence against women who are perceived to have threatened or otherwise harmed the killer's self-image. Most of these perpetrators targeted victims usually in the same age range or older than the killer; however, in the case of Cho, despite being only 15 she looked older. Since he cannot kill the actual target of his anger he finds surrogate targets who he stalks prior to the assault. Spencer punished his victims for some wrongdoing by systematically degrading, humiliating, and incapacitating them.

The next day Horgas drove to South Oxford Street where the first victim was assaulted in a nearby wooded lot after being abducted from a phone booth at South Glebe Road and Second Street in June 1983. He racked his brain trying to remember who he may have arrested nearby during that time. He and his partner Mike Hill then went through over 300 files trying to recall. Four days later the name Timmy popped into his head. Horgas remembered investigating Timmy for burglary and arson of either a house or car. On 6 January 1988 Horgas remembered Timmy's last name: Spencer. Horgas conducted a driver's license check for Timothy Spencer and found that he resided in Richmond and that he had been arrested on 29 January 1984 for a burglary in Alexandria, Virginia, just four days after police discovered Hamm's body. After serving time in prison, Spencer was released to a halfway house in the Southside area on 4 September 1987—a mere two weeks before Davis was killed. Further, Spencer's mother lived less than a mile from both murder sites in Arlington and a mere 200 yards from the Oxford Street crime scene. Horgas said that it was like a puzzle wherein all the pieces fit together perfectly. On an interesting side note, had it not been for Horgas' memory he would never have found Spencer's name in any of the parole files through which he looked so diligently as convicts released to halfway houses were not technically considered paroled.

Spencer was placed under surveillance by the Richmond Police Department; however, after a week without him doing anything suspicious the surveillance was called off. This was much to the dismay of Arlington prosecutor Helen Fahey who—not unlike Tucker—was a single woman who lived alone in a rented townhouse far too similar to Tucker's home. She contacted Horgas and the two brainstormed ideas of how to get Spencer off the street before he struck again. Fahey suggested asking for a grand jury indictment which was considerably more difficult to challenge in court that an arrest warrant.

Arrest

On 20 January 1988 at 5:50 p.m. with his grand jury indictment in hand Horgas arrested Spencer at his Richmond halfway house on suspicion of burglary.

During the drive back to Arlington, Spencer was very tight-lipped, not volunteering any statements. Horgas knew that he needed either a confession or Spencer's consent to volunteer a blood sample. Horgas asked Spencer to submit to a blood test under the guise that it was necessary to compare to some blood found on a broken window in a burglary. Unaware of the advent of DNA analysis and that a blood test could be utilized to match a semen sample, Spencer agreed, to the delight and astonishment of Horgas.

On 16 March Horgas was notified that Spencer's DNA matched fluids left at the murders of Davis, Hellams, and Tucker, as well as one of the Arlington rapes four years earlier. Both Horgas and Fahey knew they had just caught a serial killer but Fahey had to convince a jury of Spencer's guilt based upon fledgling scientific evidence that she needed jurors to understand and accept in order to obtain a capital murder conviction. In fact, due to the relative infancy and lack of knowledge about DNA evidence, trial judge Benjamin Kendrick held a special hearing to determine whether the evidence was even legally admissible. After considerable inquiry Kendrick decided that the evidence was credible and would be admitted into trial.

Trials

On 11 July 1988 Spencer went on trial in Arlington for the murder of Susan Tucker. On 16 July after only six hours of jury deliberation, Spencer was found guilty of capital murder and sentenced to death. This was the first case in the United States in which a defendant was found guilty of capital murder and received the death penalty based upon DNA evidence; a noteworthy distinction, indeed.

Spencer's Richmond trials began in the Circuit Court of the City of Richmond, Manchester Courthouse on 17 January 1989 and ultimately, on 22 September 1989, he was found guilty of rape, burglary, sodomy, and capital murder and was unanimously sentenced to death following several unsuccessful appeals of his conviction and death sentence at both state and federal levels. It didn't help his case any that when the jury was shown crime scene photos Spencer was very eager to look at them as well; essentially wanting to revisit the excitement he experienced when he brutalized the victims. Aside from this display of enthusiasm Spencer demonstrated absolutely no remorse or other emotion.

In his first appeal with Supreme Court of Virginia, Spencer raised five issues: that the DNA evidence was unreliable; that his defense team was denied the opportunity to adequately defend against said evidence because the trial court denied a discovery request for Lifecodes' notes and memoranda, that the trial court refused to provide funds for an expert DNA witness for the defense, and that the prosecution failed to reveal any evidence of problems with Lifecodes' testing process; that the trial court wrongly admitted the DNA evidence; that the prosecution improperly removed a juror for alleged racially-motivated reasons in violation of Batson v. Kentucky, 476 U.S. 79 (1986); and that the attached aggravating factor of "future dangerousness" is unconstitutionally vague. The Court upheld the lower court's ruling. The United States Supreme Court denied certiorari.

On 10 September 1990 Spencer filed a petition for a writ of habeas corpus with the state trial court which was ultimately dismissed on 15 November that same year and subsequently affirmed by the Supreme Court of Virginia. Next, Spencer filed another habeas corpus petition in the United States District Court for the Eastern District of Virginia which was also denied. He then requested a Certificate of Probable Cause to appeal which was also denied by the United States Court of Appeals, Fourth Circuit. An additional Notice of Appeal and request for Certificates of Probable Cause were filed in district court on 29 April 1993 and 25 May 1993 which were met with the respondent's motion to dismiss. The Fourth Circuit Appellate Court granted Spencer's application for Probable Cause.

In this appeal Spencer's legal team raised seven issues: ineffective assistance of counsel at the original trial because they failed to obtain a defense DNA expert; that he is "actually innocent" of the crimes for which he received the death penalty and would not have been convicted had he been able to challenge the DNA evidence and if the "prejudicial injection of astronomical probability ratios" had not been introduced at trial; that his trial counsel were ineffective due to their failure to conduct voir dire on the subject of racial prejudice; that Virginia's proportionality review is unconstitutional and does not allow "rational exceptions"; that the jury instructions regarding mitigating evidence were constitutionally inadequate; that his trial counsel were ineffective due to their failure to present certain mitigating evidence; and that the DNA analysis was unreliable, should not have been admitted, and, thus, his trial counsel were ineffective with respect to this evidence.

The Fourth Circuit considered some of Spencer's issues. First, with respect to ineffective assistance of counsel, the court turned to Strickland v. Washington, 466 U.S. 668 (1984), in which the United States Supreme Court stated that in order to prevail on an ineffective assistance of counsel claim the petitioner must demonstrate that not only did counsel perform deficiently but that the petitioner suffered prejudice as a result. Both factors must be present and the burden of proof rests with the petitioner to prove whether there was a reasonable probability that if it were not for counsel's alleged errors the result of the trial would have been different and whether there was a reasonable probability that the sentence would have concluded that other mitigating evidence would not warrant death.

Spencer's claim of ineffective assistance of counsel because of their failure to provide a defense DNA expert was dismissed due to evidence that the court not only discussed with Spencer's counsel about procuring an expert but that because no experts interviewed were willing to testify on the defense's behalf does not make his counsel ineffective. Further, his attorneys had a blind DNA test run by an independent laboratory which corroborated the evidence against Spencer.

As to the voir dire allegation of racial bias, because of the publicity surrounding Spencer's first trial in Richmond, a change of venire—wherein a jury is selected and brought in from another county due to the fear that pretrial publicity would prevent the empaneling of an impartial jury—was granted and the jury was from Norfolk. The Court held that the change of venire eliminated race as an issue with which to be concerned and that it had no reason to believe that any prospective juror had any racial bias against Spencer and this allegation was also dismissed.

With respect to the mitigating evidence concerns, Spencer contended that had his counsel adequately investigated his background that they would have discovered that his school history, presentence report, and Department of Corrections reports all stated that he was troubled; that he was emotionally damaged by being erroneously told that his father was dead when, in fact, he was not; that he regularly ingested PCP; and that he may have some degree of organic brain damage and that his counsel failed to appoint a psychologist to evaluate his mental state. The Court said that the record reflected that Spencer's counsel did, in fact, conduct a thorough background investigation which yielded evidence that Spencer's attorneys in the Arlington trial had hired both a psychiatrist and psychologist who mutually found a complete lack of any mitigating circumstances and ceased any more investigation because of fear that more incriminating evidence might have been uncovered. In fact, per the recommendation of the Richmond criminal defense bar, Dr. Robert Mullaney conducted a pretrial evaluation of Spencer and Spencer's attorneys decided to not utilize Dr. Mullaney as a witness because the sole "plus"—Mullaney's opinion that Spencer's future dangerousness would be minimized if kept in prison—was far outweighed by the potential negatives which would ensue had Dr. Mullaney testified: these being the jury finding out that Spencer committed the offense, denied his guilt, and had shown no remorse whatsoever. Further, the defense counsel stated that if they had used Dr. Mullaney then the prosecution would have been entitled to have Spencer evaluated by its own expert.

As for Spencer's claim of defense counsel's deficiency in handling adequately DNA evidence, the Court argued that his counsel did, in fact, conduct a thorough investigation and contacted several experts, some of whom assisted throughout the trial but were unwilling to testify and, therefore, determined that counsel was not ineffective simply because they could not find an expert willing to testify. Further, regarding his "actual innocence" claim and that he would not have been convicted if the "prejudicial injection of astronomical probability ratios" into the trial record had not occurred, because a claim of "actual innocence" is not a constitutional claim then—and differs from a claim of "factual innocence"— the Court's discretion was limited. Ultimately, the Court held that Spencer failed to demonstrate any constitutional error that could have affected the jury's verdict. Further, the trial judge heard all of the information regarding DNA analysis including its statistics and limitations and still decided to admit the evidence into court.

Spencer's execution date was set for 26 August 1993.

Execution

Desperate last-minute appeals for a stay of execution were denied by the United States Supreme Court and Timothy Wilson Spencer was executed on 27 April 1994. He was pronounced dead at 11:13 p.m. He was 32 at the time of his death.

Virginia author and veteran detective Lee Lofland attended Spencer's execution and described, on his website, the atmosphere at the prison as "nothing short of surreal." He stated that Spencer entered on his own, calmly took a seat in the chair, and permitted the "death squad" to secure him and attach electrodes. His face was completely devoid of any sign of fear, regret, or sadness. When asked whether Spencer had any final words it appeared that he might say something but then stopped, silently. Lofland described how Spencer made eye contact with him and even made a two-thumbs-up gesture until the leather mask was placed over his head and he was executed.

On execution day, Davis' friend Lorna Wyckoff called Spencer a "monster" and the "personification of evil." Spencer's brother Travis said it was the most difficult day of his life, hugging his brother for the last time.

Post-Execution

Whereas DNA evidence proved critical for finding Spencer guilty, it was far more difficult procuring David Vasquez's exoneration since the samples from the Hamm murder were too degraded. Vasquez would need a pardon from the governor. Fahey formerly requested the assistance of FBI Special Agent John Douglas who had founded the Behavioral Science Unit in the early 1980s after interviewing some of the most notorious serial killers in history such as Ted Bundy, Charles Manson, and David Berkowitz, and identifying patterns in their behavior; their unique "signatures." Douglas' agreement to assist was the first time FBI profilers had ever been asked to prove a suspect's innocence.

Douglas said that one must look for a signature to link similar cases and that a signature was a type of ritual performed by a suspect that is truly unique. Douglas believed that the nature of how Spencer bound his victims constituted a distinctive signature in the five homicides and that use of ligatures and ropes exceeded the necessary amount of force necessary to control the victims was also part of his signature. On 4 January 1989 Vasquez was pardoned and became the first person exonerated, albeit indirectly, by DNA evidence.

Spencer's conviction was such a landmark case because it broadened the public and professional knowledge about DNA and that the jury understood its significance and was able to convict a serial killer of capital murder was a major revelation. The case also prompted Virginia to open the first state DNA laboratory in the United States in 1989 and to set up the first DNA database.

Shortly thereafter, in 1992, the Innocence Project came into being. A nonprofit founded by New York's Benjamin Cardozo School of Law, the Innocence Project has worked to free 179 of the 337 people exonerated by DNA evidence, including 20 who were on death row. The most common reason cited for wrongful convictions is erroneous eyewitness identification with mishandling of forensic evidence due to faulty tests and/or procedural errors the second reason. DNA is not completely infallible, however. The Innocence Project states that approximately four percent of those exonerated were originally convicted as a result of improperly conducted DNA tests which have prompted virtually all defense attorneys in criminal proceedings to request retesting on their clients' behalf.

In addition to Paul Mones' (1995) book Stalking Justice: The Dramatic True Story of the Detective Who First Used DNA

Testing to Catch a Serial Killer that focused upon Detective Horgas' efforts to link his cases in Arlington to those in Richmond and, ultimately, to Spencer, Spencer's case provided the basis for Patricia Cornwell's first crime novel Postmortem (1990) as she, at the time was employed as a computer analyst in the Richmond, Virginia's Office of the Chief Medical Examiner. Former FBI profiler John Douglas devoted chapter 11 of his 1996 memoir Journey into Darkness to Spencer. His case also inspired the forensic science documentary Medical Detectives which first aired on 31 October 1996.